Praise for The *Art of You*

"*The Art of You* embodies the message that creativity is the highest form of healing, which has been beyond true in my life and in many others'. If you're looking for an alternative to the density of the typical spiritual path and to transmute your obstacles into your masterpieces, this book is for you."

Sahara Rose
bestselling author, host of *Highest Self Podcast*

"Every time I talk to James, I walk away feeling inspired. Even though I've been an artist my entire life, James still makes me think about my creative path in new ways. When you read *The Art of You*, it's like talking with James. You'll feel his wise, playful, and powerful creative guidance—and be left feeling like a whole new universe of possibilities has opened within you."

Cory Allen
host of *And Then It Hit Me* podcast, author of *Now Is the Way*

"*The Art of You* is an inspiring, pragmatic, and uplifting guide to creating fulfilling art and a fulfilling life."

Tao Lin
novelist, poet, bestselling author

"Besides meditation, creativity is one of the main focuses of my life, and I have found it to be a playful and exacting art. *The Art of You* offers great insights and steps on how to cultivate creativity and allow it to flow forth. This is essential reading for all looking to share their unique experience, to foster deep connections, and to inspire others."

Yung Pueblo
#1 *New York Times* bestselling author

"*The Art of You* made me feel like a kid again, ready to throw paint on a canvas when I've spent my adult life terrified of the blank page. James McCrae demystifies the creative process, making it accessible to everyone with his practical tools and tips. His work feels like gentle encouragement, bringing both playfulness and depth into what it means to be an artist."

Allie Michelle
poet, bestselling author, co-founder of wellness
and writing community We Are Warriors

"*The Art of You* is a poetic journey into finding your artistic voice and learning how to express it with passion and power."

IN-Q
award-winning poet and performer, multi-platinum songwriter

"*The Art of You* shows us where our creativity and humanity intersect, and how getting to the core of both can transform our lives on a fundamental level. James McCrae flawlessly demonstrates what propels the heart of creativity and how to become more in touch with our own."

Brianna Pastor
poet, mental health advocate, author of *Good Grief*

"The most powerful decision any of us can make is to live in devotion to healthily experiencing the all-ness that life wants to bring our way. *The Art of You* shares how to do this and bursts the door wide open for you to make your truest and greatest ripple in the eternal now."

Alyson Charles Storey
shaman, bestselling author of *Animal Power*,
host of *Ceremony Circle* podcast

THE
ART
OF YOU

Also by James McCrae

Sh#t Your Ego Says

*How to Laugh in Ironic Amusement
During Your Existential Crisis*

THE
ART
OF YOU

THE ESSENTIAL GUIDEBOOK FOR

RECLAIMING YOUR CREATIVITY

JAMES McCRAE

sounds true
BOULDER, COLORADO

Sounds True
Boulder, CO

Sounds True is a trademark of Sounds True, Inc.

Published 2024

Cover design by James McCrae
Jacket design by Lisa Kerans
Book design by Meredith Jarrett
Illustrations © 2024 James McCrae

Printed in Canada

BK06737

Library of Congress Cataloging-in-Publication Data
Names: McCrae, James, 1982- author.
Title: The art of you : the essential guidebook for reclaiming your
    creativity / James McCrae.
Description: Boulder, Colorado : Sounds True, 2024. | Includes
    bibliographical references.
Identifiers: LCCN 2023007556 (print) | LCCN 2023007557 (ebook) | ISBN
    9781649631466 (paperback) | ISBN 9781649631473 (ebook)
Subjects: LCSH: Creative ability.
Classification: LCC BF408 .M33527 2024 (print) | LCC BF408 (ebook) | DDC
    153.3/5--dc23/eng/20230624
LC record available at https://lccn.loc.gov/2023007556
LC ebook record available at https://lccn.loc.gov/2023007557

10 9 8 7 6 5 4 3 2 1

Dedicated to my creative teachers:

Walt Whitman, Allen Ginsberg, Bob Dylan, Joan Didion,
Jean-Michel Basquiat, Patti Smith, Andy Warhol, David Bowie,
Jack Kerouac, Mary Oliver, Gabriel García Márquez,
John and Alice Coltrane, Rick Rubin, Jay-Z, William S. Burroughs,
Hafiz, Hilma af Klint, Tupac Shakur, Saul Williams, Sophie Strand,
Emma Zeck, Alex and Allyson Gray, Arthur Rimbaud, Taylor Swift, Lou
Reed, Pharrell Williams, Haruki Murakami, Terence McKenna, Hunter
S. Thompson, Charles Bukowski, Prince, Ernest Hemingway, Paul
Rand, Marcel Duchamp, Lana Del Rey, Bunny Michael,
David Lynch, Anthony Bourdain, Daniel Johnston, Gabi Abrão,
Hanna Williams, Lao Tzu, Conor Oberst, Seth Godin, Tyler the Creator,
Sahara Rose, Frida Kahlo, Pablo Picasso, Tao Lin, Virgil Abloh,
Henry Miller, Chelsie Diane, Frank Ocean, William Blake,
Miles Davis, Yoko Ono, and more.

CONTENTS

Foreword by Lalah Delia   xi

Introduction: Start Where You Are   1

PART ONE: Yin: Creative Being

Chapter 1: The Art of Doing Nothing   13

Chapter 2: Setting an Intention   25

Chapter 3: Guides and Inspiration   37

Chapter 4: Cultivating Intuition   49

Chapter 5: Creativity and Emotion: A Love Story   63

Chapter 6: Imagination: Seeing with Your Third Eye   75

Chapter 7: Intervention with My Inner Critic   91

PART TWO: Yang: Creative Doing

Chapter 8: The Myth of Perfection   99

Chapter 9: Finding Your Style   115

Chapter 10: Inspiration Is a Habit   129

Chapter 11: Experimentation and Play   143

Chapter 12: Launching Your Work   157

Chapter 13: Going Pro   173

Chapter 14: The New Renaissance:
                    Creativity and Social Impact   189

WORKSHOP: Your Creative Signature

What's Your Creative Signature?   213

Afterword: Creativity Is Your Nature   223

"Sing Along" (a Poem)   226

Bibliography   235

About the Author   243

"I feel like I'm channeling ideas from somewhere else. I believe we all are. I believe we are vehicles for information. When it's ready to come through, it comes through. And the people who have good antennas pick up the signal."

– Rick Rubin

CREATIVE TRAILMARKERS
(IN CASE YOU GET LOST)

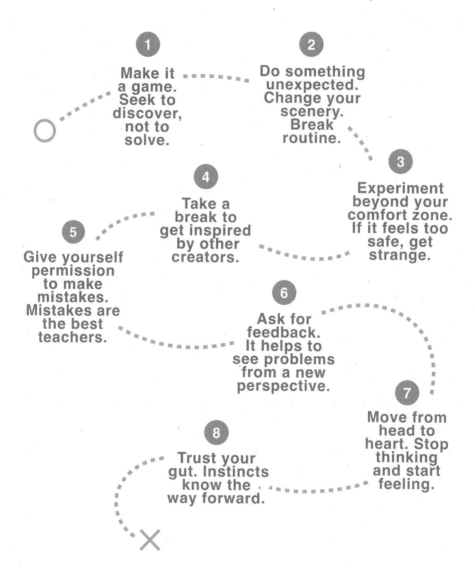

1 Make it a game. Seek to discover, not to solve.

2 Do something unexpected. Change your scenery. Break routine.

3 Experiment beyond your comfort zone. If it feels too safe, get strange.

4 Take a break to get inspired by other creators.

5 Give yourself permission to make mistakes. Mistakes are the best teachers.

6 Ask for feedback. It helps to see problems from a new perspective.

7 Move from head to heart. Stop thinking and start feeling.

8 Trust your gut. Instincts know the way forward.

FOREWORD

by Lalah Delia

MUCH LIKE THE hero's journey, the journey of creativity is filled with obstacles, challenges, and moments of life-changing victory. The path from idea to materialization can feel like navigating the unknown and slaying dragons along the way. Taking risks and staying resilient are essential. It's not enough to simply have a good idea; you must also be willing to take what's deep within you and work with it—*create with it*. You eventually become soft enough to notice the lessons your life is giving you and strong enough to remain audacious and optimistic against all odds. Creativity brings out our otherworldly nature. It summons our inner hero (and shero) to respond.

It all started with a simple quote: "She remembered who she was, and the game changed." I wrote these words in my journal while going through a divorce and soon after decided to share them with the world. Little did I know that this small act of courage would take me on a journey I am still exploring today.

Creativity is more than recreation or a hobby; it's alchemy. And it has been an extraordinary path of healing and metamorphosis in my life.

On my own creative shero's journey, I've uncovered who I am and become more whole. Deep wounds and inner blocks have dissolved. Years of trauma and pain were put to rest. I found my voice, my truth, and a new life. Fear and all, I allowed myself to rise from the ashes and live courageously, authentically, and more expansively. I discovered more of the Divine's presence in my life. I cleared looping cycles of wandering in the dark. And somewhere along the way, I arrived at an opening to higher dimensions of creativity, expression, and experience.

I began to realize that creativity is a path of honoring and unlocking more of who you are as an instrument and conduit as you allow the force of the muse to channel through and guide you. It's meeting more of yourself and evolving as you go. The opposite of this is how I felt for a long time, living in stagnation and creative deprivation. Allowing creativity to flow through you is the same as allowing yourself to live more fully and freely. It's a force leading to deeper purpose and fulfillment.

It's not just about making great things; it's about embracing why you are alive. It's about standing in your power, owning your story, and realizing you have something unique to contribute. It's about uncovering the beauty, medicine, and humor in everyday life that no one sees until you courageously and uniquely present it to them.

James McCrae is a master at this very thing.

Through the power of his writing, memes, and art, he offers us laughter, contemplation, comfort, and deep insights. He is a force leading us to higher realms of creative purpose.

As you take this journey into the unknown, with James as your guide, you are already winning. Ahhh, this is a great place to exhale in relief. Together, you'll explore the creative process and what being an "artist" actually means. You will gain insight into maintaining a healthy balance between discipline and flow. James will lead you to an awareness that with creativity comes power, purpose, and connection.

This book is about breaking down old paradigms that may have been holding you back in both life and creativity.

Becoming the creative hero of your story is a shift from the perpetual state of seeking yourself and committing to the journey of self-creation. And with this shift, I decided to take control of my life and move forward with a fresh outlook and renewed courage.

Each step I took was about learning to trust myself and the process, take action despite fear, and embrace change, even when it felt awkward and uncomfortable. The process wasn't always easy, but it showed me that anything is possible when you find the strength to take the next step into the unknown. Looking back at my journey, I can see how valuable it has been and how much I've grown and expanded along the way.

Whether or not you see creativity as a mystical, divine force—as I do—it will help you harness the power to open doors to opportunities you never knew existed.

During my senior year in high school, I was awarded a rare scholarship from a prestigious design university. My creative dreams of attending this school came to an abrupt halt when I realized I was unable to afford housing. I was devastated. But with higher purpose and self-determination, I went on to become a multidisciplinary creative artist, touching lives worldwide. I've written a bestselling book and have been featured in my teenage favorite, *Vogue Magazine*, numerous times—as well as an array of broadcast media from cool underground to major media coverage ranging from podcasts to national television. And still a highlight to me, my writing was featured on a billboard in the heart of Times Square for the entirety of Mental Health Awareness Month. Alongside flashing billboards promoting consumer capitalism were little notes of soul medicine for people passing by:

This is all temporary, love yourself through it.

Your boundaries attract the right type of people.

Keep taking time for yourself until you're you again.

In response to this placement, James commented on social media, "Quotes by Lalah Delia in Times Square is the type of advertisement we need."

I've since learned that this coveted placement costs between $5,000 and $50,000 a day. A DAY!! To have my work featured in Times Square for thirty days at zero cost to me (after all I've overcome) has been an enormous blessing and an actual example of one of my favorite quotes by James: "Be the glitch you want to see in the matrix."

Talk about full circle. After being cast off by some (and, at times, by myself) as never being likely to make a career of inspiring souls, what they say is true: never give up on your dreams. And to that I'll add: never give up on your gifts and higher purpose because they will take you places you never imagined.

Create your own path and version of success. You are capable of so much more than you may realize. The sky really is the limit when you don't let anyone (including yourself) put a glass ceiling over you.

This book is an invitation to reclaim your inherent creativity. May you become the creative force you are meant to be.

Lalah Delia
bestselling author, founder of Vibrate Higher Daily

TO MAKE
LIVING ITSELF
AN ART,
THAT IS
THE GOAL

— HENRY MILLER

Introduction

START WHERE YOU ARE

TO BE HUMAN is to be creative. You don't have to be a professional artist or blessed with rare talents. Having the ability to tap into an invisible realm to imagine something that doesn't exist—and then to shape and bend the material world to make your imagination real—is perhaps the most defining characteristic of being human.

The act of creation (making something out of nothing) is equivalent to magic, and each person is a magician. This is true for the accountant as much as the artist. To be alive is to be in a state of constant cocreation with the universe. We create our relationships, our careers, our home environments, our routines, our belief systems, and the messages we share with the world, which we broadcast, either subtly or overtly, in every conversation and social media post.

Art is not restricted to traditional mediums like painting or literature. Being an artist isn't about fitting into a predefined template. It's about returning to your nature, being an independent thinker, and actualizing your unique purpose. Creativity is natural. The same way a bee's nature is to make honey and an apple tree's nature is to grow apples, it is human nature to create. It is an energy that flows through us.

A podcast can be art. Social media content can be art. Creating and marketing your business is art. Music and fashion are art. Memes are art.

Hosting a dinner party can be art. Developing an app is art. Even if you don't make anything tangible, you create your life. You make your career, your relationships, your home. When done with intention, even sex is art. An artist is anyone who uses the power of imagination and creativity to birth a new idea into existence. You create your life in each passing moment. The question is: *Are you creating with conscious intention, or are you reacting to external circumstances and creating by default?*

As we grow up, it becomes increasingly difficult to live and work from a place of intuition and curiosity. Society doesn't always support our natural creative talents. Being an artist, we are told, is not realistic. It is a privilege reserved for the chosen few. We are taught to follow rules, conform to social conventions, and work to support top-down power structures instead of investing our energy toward actualizing our own unique visions for the purpose of healing and evolving ourselves and the world around us.

We are each born on a mission to manifest the most authentic expression of ourselves. But millions of gears in the socioeconomic machine are engineered to make us disempowered and forget who we truly are. Our magic is real, but we've been taught all the wrong tricks.

The creative initiation.

These days, many people feel lost or disoriented because society fails to provide them with meaningful initiations. "Go to college; get a job" is the prevailing rite of passage into adulthood. But this pseudo-initiation feels shallow. We are told that finding a profession is more important than finding a purpose. Instead of advancing to the next level of an empowering game, we shrink ourselves to fit into socially constructed boxes.

Creative people in particular suffer from a lack of meaningful initiation. In a world where data and productivity are valued over imagination, it's often difficult for writers, artists, and creatives to find their place. More often than not, creative people compromise their natural gifts in order to function within the factory of society. And while we may maintain a creative project as a hobby, it's likely that we will dedicate less and less time to these passions as the pressures and demands of "real life" take center stage.

Although we are all born with creative potential, creativity and inspiration are like muscles: we have to nurture them or they will atrophy. The good news is that it's never too late to reawaken the curious artist and child inside. But without an established social road map to help us walk the creative path, it's up to us as individuals to make a personal commitment to nurture the gifts of imagination and expression.

This book is a road map for the creative journey. Of course, a definitive rule book is impossible. After all, creativity is a living phenomenon. There are no absolute rules. It's about capturing the spirit in the moment and following where it leads you. What works for me might not work for you. What works today might not work tomorrow. Like a spontaneous jazz band, creativity is about awareness and action in the moment— trusting yourself to take small leaps of faith again and again.

After decades of trial and error, I've gradually discovered the keys to conscious and consistent creativity. Each creative process follows certain stages. To master these stages is to enter a state of effortless flow. These stages can be broken down into two main categories: yin and yang. Yin is about *creative being*: setting an intention, finding creative guides, having a curious mind, and cultivating intuition and imagination, which we'll cover in part one. Yang is about *creative doing*: finding your voice, experimenting with technique, launching projects, growing an audience, and making an impact, which we'll cover in part two.

In our materialistic, yang society, the conventional wisdom is to focus on the end result first. If only we can *have* what we want, then we can *do* what we want, and finally we can *be* who we want. But the opposite is true. If we want to *have*, first we must *do*. And before we can *do*, we must *be*. All doing is born from presence. All having is born from being.

Cultivating inner presence is the first step of creativity. But it's not the last step. We must also take action to create, experiment with technique, edit our work, and find the courage to share. Each of these stages requires a different approach. The open-minded, intuitive yin that inspires an idea is not necessarily the best mindset to drive that idea to fruition.

The creative process is similar to farming. First you must prepare the soil, gather and plant seeds, and nurture the sprouts with water and sunlight. These are yin activities. The soil represents the fertile subconscious. The seeds are the influences we feed ourselves: the books we read, the music we listen to, and the people we surround ourselves with. The soil of our subconscious mind will inevitably produce the fruits of the seeds we plant. These fruits are our thoughts and ideas.

Once the crops are grown, an entirely new set of actions is needed. We must harvest the crops, clean and store them, and eventually cook them into a meal that can be served and enjoyed. These are yang activities. The crops are our ideas. We clean and store them by choosing which ideas to develop. Cooking a meal is the art of creative execution, which requires time and patience to learn. And finally, we need to take our work public. After all, art, like food, is meant to be shared and enjoyed—to provide nourishment and pleasure to others.

According to traditional Chinese medicine, when one aspect of the body is out of alignment, the entire body may suffer or break down as a result. The same is true of the creative process. Creativity is a living energy that flows through us. When the energy gets stuck in one place, the whole process breaks down.

Different people get stuck in different places. Some people have vivid imaginations but are unable to finish and launch projects. Others may be superproductive, but their work is lacking the purpose and depth that comes from intuition. No matter where you are on your creative journey, this book is designed to help you return to alignment and flow.

THE ART OF YOU

> "Every child is an artist. The problem is how to remain an artist once he grows up."

PABLO PICASSO

How this book came to be.

I've been an artist my whole life, starting with my childhood in a small Minnesota town. Sometimes I've been paid for my work. Sometimes I've done it only because I had no other choice—something inside me wanted to come out. I've created advertising campaigns for big brands, and I've scrawled poetry during my lunch break while working odd jobs making minimum wage. I've graduated from art school and worked as a professional graphic designer. I've filled stacks of note-books with musings that nobody will ever read, and I've created memes that have gone viral around the world. I've been a starving artist, and I've led advertising teams on Madison Avenue. I've been rejected by countless book publishers, and I've written bestselling books that were translated into languages around the world. I've been a painter, recorded a spoken-word poetry album, made more mistakes than I can count, and gradually learned how to grow an audience and turn my creativity into a business. Today, I work with clients and teach classes on conscious creativity. I'm also the founder and host of Sunflower Club, a podcast and global community dedicated to creativity as a tool for personal healing and social transformation. All of these experiences—though not always successful—were instrumental in shaping who I am as a human and a creator. And somewhere along the way, I learned how to claim the identity of an artist.

While living in New York City and working in the advertising indus-try, my creativity hit a dead end. My open-minded curiosity had been replaced by tight deadlines and office politics. But I rediscovered my inner artist when I began exploring mindfulness and spirituality, including meditation, yoga, Eastern philosophy, and the teachings of Ram Dass, Terence McKenna, and Alan Watts. Seeking to balance my busy outer world, I began a diligent mindfulness practice, often sitting in meditation for hours at a time. Eventually I started attending plant medicine ceremonies led by shamans from Peru and Mexico, working with psychedelic substances like psilocybin and ayahuasca.

Everything changed. I realized that my creative process had become too one-dimensional. In Taoist terms, there was too much yang (force and effort) and not enough yin (allowing and flow). So I began to slow down and cultivate a receptive presence within myself. My channel of inspiration opened wider than ever. Instead of standing in a small, shallow pond, I was swimming in a vast, deep ocean.

Perhaps the most important lesson my creative journey has taught me is to recognize and honor creativity as a sacred path unto itself. This path isn't about having tremendous talent, perfect technique, or an impressive education. It's about unlearning the limitations and conditioning that separate us from our intrinsic and spontaneous creative nature. This nature—no matter how far away we have strayed—is always within our grasp, one shift in perception away.

Creativity is more important than ever.

Our world is quickly changing. The rate of novelty, driven by technology and social disruption, is accelerating each year. With increased change comes increased uncertainty. The comfortable known has been replaced with a vast and murky unknown.

This uncertainty can cause us to freeze in fear and confusion, unsure which direction to take. What worked in the past is not guaranteed to work in the future. We need new ways of thinking, working, and living. This is a call for radical creativity—an opportunity to imagine, design, and build the future we want to see. We need creativity now more than ever.

Creativity is about being an independent thinker. You don't need tremendous talent; you just need the courage to question conventional wisdom. Your life isn't a movie that you're watching. It's a game that you're playing—a game that's fluid and ever changing. There are no rules, just a collection of socially reinforced agreements.

> "You never change things by fighting the existing reality. To change something, build a new model that makes the existing model obsolete."

BUCKMINSTER FULLER

Creativity represents the freedom to think for ourselves instead of following the rules bestowed upon us by others. Every valuable contribution to society came about by taking risks and dreaming outside the collective comfort zone. Creativity is the key that opens doors to new businesses, new relationships, new communities, new politics, and new solutions. Without the key, we are subject to the authority of social conventions. With the key, we become magicians, casting spells to align our lives with our soul's calling.

You are an artist (yes, you).

In the age of the internet, social media, and decentralized platforms like podcasting and live streaming, each person is an influencer and media channel unto themselves. More than ever before, we are living in public, broadcasting our thoughts and ideas to the world. This rapidly changing media landscape has huge implications on how we communicate, do business, and make and consume art.

The line between art and artist is starting to blur. The content creator is just as important as the content. In both business and art, authenticity is more important than ever. Your brand is your message, and your message is you. In the digital age, creativity is about establishing a real and direct relationship with your audience. The more honest and vulnerable you can be, the better. Your authenticity is your currency. The lessons in this book will help you step out of the closet as an artist, a thinker, and a creator.

All artists—in fact, all people—are transmitters of vibration. Imagination and intuition are antennas that pick up signals from unseen dimensions and download messages to the hard drive of conscious thought. The mind then works with the body—activating hands, fingers, and vocal cords—to share the transmission as creative expression. We are carriers for the thoughts, ideas, and art that pass through us.

If you feel a desire to create, to share, to step up and be seen and heard, this isn't an accident. There is an energy, a transmission, that has selected you to deliver its message. Making art (whatever art you choose) and cultivating your creative genius are about living in service to your higher purpose. To discover and embody this purpose is the sacred mission of your life.

We often take our own gifts for granted. But here's the truth: the world needs what you have to share. Somebody out there is looking for the exact message that comes naturally to you. People are starving for authenticity, for something real. Nobody else can replicate the energy you offer. Your words, your art, and your being are medicine for the world.

Art is alchemy. It transmutes pain into beauty. When we create art, we open a tiny portal to the soul that brings light to a world of darkness. And in doing so, we give others permission to do the same. It's time to boldly share your vision with the world.

We are waiting for your transmission.

I AM ALIVE TO:

☐ Follow the rules, go to college, get a job, fit in, hide my light, and live safely inside a box.

☑ Remember and actualize my higher purpose by waking up to my inherent creative nature as a living miracle inside a human body.

A JOURNEY INTO THE UNKNOWN

The creative process is like going for a midnight walk in a dark forest with a flashlight and no map. You can't see the end from the beginning. Each turn reveals a new mystery, a new surprise.

At times you may feel lost or afraid. That's okay. Getting lost is part of the process. Let yourself wander. Wandering leads to wondering. And wondering leads to revelation.

All art is a work in progress. Just like you. You don't have to have it all figured out. The path is revealed as you stumble forward one step at a time.

We're all making it up as we go.

PART ONE

YIN: CREATIVE BEING

Chapter 1

THE ART OF DOING NOTHING

"Nature does not hurry,
yet everything is accomplished."

LAO TZU

ISLANDS ARE TYPICALLY known for their tranquility. The proximity to water has a calming effect; the tide's ebb and flow is a reminder that all things come and go at nature's pace. But the island of Manhattan, where the ocean is blocked by highways, seems immune to this effect. The modern incarnation of Manahatta (the lush, wilderness home of the Indigenous Lenape people) hardly seems like an island at all but rather an experimental, urban fishbowl, thirteen miles long and two miles wide.

Businessmen rush to meetings. Hare Krishnas chant holy incantations in Union Square. Teenagers dance on subways for spare change. Tourists carry designer shopping bags down SoHo cobblestone streets. Homeless people sleep on benches in Central Park. The traffic, bumper to bumper from Brooklyn Bridge to the Bronx, feels like the collective state of mind reflected in steel, aluminum, and concrete. Everyone is trying to get ahead, inch by inch, toward some urgent destination.

As for me, I was an ambitious young professional working for an ad agency on Madison Avenue. My days consisted of packed subway rides, strong coffee, and back-to-back client meetings. As a creative strategist, my job was to help brands gain an edge over their competition. I conducted research, facilitated client workshops, led brainstorms, and helped develop value propositions, taglines, digital strategies, and marketing campaigns. I was usually working with multiple clients at the same time. Deadlines were always tight.

It was a "work hard, party hard" culture. To make up for the long working hours, alcohol started flowing through the office around five or six each evening. We'd usually work for a couple more hours and then head to a crowded Manhattan bar for more drinks (and often cocaine) before getting a few hours of sleep and starting over the next day. We were making a lot of money. We were very productive. We were also exhausted, and a deep and thinly veiled sadness was lurking below the surface.

One winter evening I was finishing my work and preparing to go drinking with coworkers. My plans changed when I received a text from a friend inviting me to the Rubin Museum of Art for a lecture on Taoism, something I didn't know much about. Deciding to give it a chance, I left the office, hailed a cab, and watched snow fall over Manhattan as we drove to West 17th Street.

We took off our coats and entered the auditorium. There was a peaceful energy in the room—much different from the frantic pace in my office. On stage, an older Chinese man sat quietly in a chair, waiting to be interviewed. My friend and I sat in the back of the room. I was happy to have opted out of another night of drinking to nurture my mind and soul.

Taoism, I learned, is a philosophy that emerged from ancient Chinese shamanism, and it is the precursor to Buddhism. According to Taoism, everything that exists can be traced back to a mysterious energy source called the Tao. All of nature lives, grows, changes, and dies in accordance with the wisdom of the Tao, which keeps the universe balanced in perfect harmony.

Unlike many religions, Taoism doesn't attempt to personify this phenomenon. There is no God, no watchful eye in the sky. The Tao is unknowable, similar to Native American traditions that refer to creation as simply the Great Mystery. *The Tao that can be named is not the true Tao*, according to one of the key principles of Taoism. Although the Tao doesn't have a name or a face, it does have a nature. And this nature permeates all things, including people. Taoism teaches that when we align ourselves with the delicate ebb and flow of the Tao, we will live in peaceful harmony with our own nature and the nature of the world around us.

"The Tao's nature is to create," the man on stage said, "and therefore it is human nature to create. But creativity, like all things, requires a balance of yin and yang. There is a time to reap and a time to sow. A time to produce and a time to receive. When we are aligned with our own nature, which is a microcosm of all nature, creativity is effortless."

A light bulb turned on inside my head. I suddenly realized why I was feeling anxious and uninspired. My creativity was one sided: all force, no flow. I was hustling to meet deadlines, drinking too much coffee and alcohol, playing office politics, and working from a place of *unconscious reactivity* rather than *conscious creativity*. By any external measure, I was successful. But something important was missing. I was overworked and uninspired. I had lost my connection to intuition, to curiosity, to wonder, and ultimately to myself. I was trying to fill every minute with productivity, which wasn't natural. Flowers can't remain in evergreen bloom. They need periods of rest and restoration to support new growth.

When I got back to my Upper East Side apartment, I ordered the Tao Te Ching, a poetic treatise on Taoism attributed to a sage named Lao Tzu. Little by little, I learned how to apply the principles of Taoism to my life and my career. I learned that rest and restoration are just as important as work and productivity. I gave myself more space to think, to daydream, to do nothing. I replaced my evening drinking routine with yoga and meditation. I started cultivating my own inner presence instead of always reacting to external circumstances. And gradually my inspiration started to flourish again.

Reawakening the yin.

Perhaps the most important lesson I learned from Taoism is the dualistic principle of yin and yang, which explains the Tao by breaking down its mysterious nature into two equal and opposite parts. Yin is the passive principle. Represented by the color black, yin is the feminine nature of the universe that remains in a state of open receptivity. Yang is the active principle. Represented by the color white, yang is the masculine nature of the universe that initiates action with force. These two sides are not in conflict with each other. They complement and depend on each other. In the natural world, yin and yang exist in perfect balance, representing the eternal dance of polarity.

One example of yin and yang working together can be seen in a river. The water represents the flowing yin, the feminine. The banks of the river represent the order and structure of yang, the masculine. Without the water, the banks would have no meaning. Without the banks, the river would overflow into a flood. But together, the water flows with purpose and direction.

YIN QUALITIES	YANG QUALITIES
Being	Doing
Flow	Structure
Femininity	Masculinity
Feeling	Thinking
Dreaming	Making
Receptivity	Action
Intuition	Logic
Spiritual	Physical

It's important to note that, while yin represents the feminine archetype and yang represents the masculine archetype, these qualities are not exclusive to any gender. Every male, female, and nonbinary person contains both yin and yang energy. Nature is not complete without both, and neither are we.

When yin is missing, a person might be focused and productive, but their work will lack intuitive awareness and depth of feeling. When yang is missing, a person might be deeply emotional and intuitive, but they will struggle to finish and launch projects. We require the balanced integration of yin and yang to reach our fullest potential as humans and creators.

In the natural world, yin and yang are equally important. They depend on each other for stability and balance. However, in modern civilization, the two are not always treated equally. For thousands of years, yang has been placed on a pedestal while yin has been suppressed.

Yin is a fertile garden that grows in accordance with nature. Modern society, by contrast, operates more like a factory. Action and productivity are valued above all else. Yin qualities such as patience, intuition, and wisdom have been marginalized in favor of yang qualities like rationality, materialism, and competition.

There is nothing wrong with yang, with masculine energy, or with being action oriented, but without the counterbalance of yin, our actions will lack depth and purpose. Instead of nurturing, we push. Instead of listening, we react. Instead of rehabilitating, we punish. Instead of engaging conflict with compassion and empathy, we wage war. This radical imbalance has inflicted untold trauma on women for centuries, while suppressing the yin inside us all.

The overemphasis on action-oriented yang has drawn our collective attention away from the sacred inner world, the dark and mysterious yin, the pregnant womb that nurtures imagination and gives birth to creativity. Yin doesn't demand constant force or action. It only asks that we remain still and listen to the quiet, knowing voice of our nature. When we are grounded in yin, our actions come from a place of purpose and depth.

Yin and creativity.

In terms of creativity, yin is about listening, receiving, contemplating, and allowing ourselves to simply *be* without pressure to act or produce. A good example of artists who emphasize yin are Japanese haiku writers who spend countless hours observing nature only to produce a simple, seventeen-syllable poem. It isn't the quantity of words or fancy style of language that matters; it is the depth of awareness. The output is a tiny reflection of a deep relationship with nature.

"An old silent pond.

A frog jumps into the pond—

Splash! Silence again."

BASHŌ

Another example is the writer Mary Oliver. In her poems and essays, she invites the reader to slow down and appreciate natural beauty. She is never in a hurry to make a point. Like the natural world itself, her writing ebbs and flows to reach a natural conclusion. Reading Oliver taught me to get out of my own head and pay attention to details. Whether she's writing about walking in the forest, playing with her dogs, or contemplating the changing seasons, her words feel like a natural extension of her breath. For Oliver, observation is its own reward. "Sometimes I need only to stand wherever I am to be blessed," she wrote.

When the poet Allen Ginsberg was asked if he spent a lot of time polishing his poems, he said no, but that he did spend a lot of time polishing his mind. What he meant was that his writing process involved sitting in meditation and contemplation until the words naturally arose like flowers from the soil. His writing was a direct dictation of his natural awareness with minimal interference.

Yin can't be forced. It's about flow and receptivity, setting aside the ego's agenda, to be guided by a higher wisdom. The more deeply we listen to nature and intuition, the more clarity and power our words will carry when we finally speak.

> **"I think I will do nothing for a long time but listen."**

WALT WHITMAN

Be here now.

Creativity isn't something we need to learn. The problem is that we have been trained by society to suppress our creative gifts. We are taught that productivity is more important than imagination, that following rules is more important than following intuition. Instilled at a young age, these lessons harden into mental blocks that keep us from living in creative flow.

The first step of creativity is not about making things. The first step is about unlearning the social programming that separates us from our creative nature. It's about lowering the volume on the nagging voice of external expectations and attuning our awareness to the inner voice of intuition and imagination.

Energy is sacred. When we give away our energy and attention, we give away our power. Living a creative life requires us to cultivate a sense of presence and power within. This means being attentive to the needs of the body. It means giving ourselves the time and space to reclaim our consciousness so we can create with purpose and intention.

There's an expression in Chinese, *wu wei*, which roughly translates to "doing nothing." Wu wei is not about total inaction. It's about aligning our actions with the flow of nature. The concept of wu wei is expressed in Taoism: *The Tao does nothing, yet nothing remains undone.*

In our fast-paced society, doing nothing is not as easy as it sounds. We are trained to glorify productivity. How many times have you asked someone how they've been doing and heard the response "I've been super busy" as a point of pride? Our worth is too often measured by our external accomplishments. Doing nothing, we are told, is lazy and selfish.

Even our leisure time is consumed with doing. We relax by watching TV, listening to podcasts, and engaging in recreational activities. The mind and body rarely get a chance to slow down and enter a space of pure contemplation. Doing nothing not only goes against our capitalistic conditioning, it also goes against our altruistic impulses. Rest and relaxation, it seems, are a waste of time when we could be helping others. But the truth is that self-care is medicine for the world. We have to take care of ourselves before we're in a position to effectively take care of those around us. An empty cup cannot fill others.

I eventually quit my job in advertising and left New York City with my girlfriend to live in the scenic wildlife of Topanga Canyon on the outskirts of Los Angeles. After a season of stress and stimulation, it was time for a season of salt water, sunlight, and healing. I started writing poetry again. We adopted two dogs. And I spent many hours hiking, swimming, and basking in the sun.

The COVID-19 pandemic began shortly after I arrived in California, followed by a global quarantine. Activity around the world ground to a halt. Though this was a painful and confusing time, the forced period of rest led to a sense of collective relief. Instead of going into the office, many people started working from home, giving them a chance to slow down and reflect on their lives and priorities.

These days, I try not to force my creative process. I do my best to listen to my body, feel my emotions, and trust my intuition. There's a time to push and a time to let go, a time to speak and a time to listen, a time to hurry and a time to daydream. The demands of modern life don't always allow us to rest for long periods of time. There is always another project, another deadline. We need to find ways to carve out time for yin, to make rest and contemplation a priority, even if only for a few minutes or hours at a time. This means breaking the toxic bonds with society that tell us to always push, push, push in the name of productivity. When we calm the nervous system and slow down our busy thoughts, we tune into the wisdom of stillness.

CREATIVE PLAYTIME

One day of nothing

The art of doing nothing is about getting into alignment with your inner nature. At the beginning, this might be uncomfortable. For many of us, the voice of external obligations is louder than the quiet voice of inner wisdom. The "one day of nothing" ritual is about giving yourself full permission to practice the art of nondoing without guilt for one full day.

Guidelines for your day of nothing:

- Choose a day when you will have the fewest distractions

- Spend the day in silence, preferably in nature

- Take a break from screens (television, computer, phone)

- Refrain from productivity—even if you feel the urge to work

- Let yourself stare off into space and daydream

- Listen to your body to understand what movement and nourishment it needs

- At the end of the day, write down your reflections

Read the Tao Te Ching

One of the oldest books in existence, the Tao Te Ching is a wellspring of poetic insight into the mysterious and contradictory nature of the universe. Find a copy (my favorite translation is by Stephen Mitchell, but each translation offers a unique flavor) and take your time reading it. Allow yourself to sit in quiet contemplation, letting each passage sink in before moving on. Return to the book whenever you need to recharge.

A few other books that may help you slow down and return to the present moment include *Be Here Now* by Ram Dass, *The Gift* by Hafiz, *Devotions* by Mary Oliver, and *The Power of Now* by Eckhart Tolle.

THE YIN & YANG OF CREATIVITY

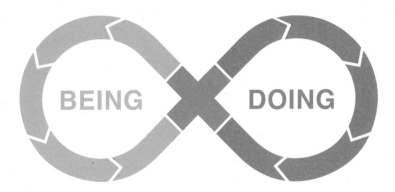

BEING	DOING
BEING CURIOUS	ACTUALIZING YOUR IDEAS
GIVING YOURSELF SPACE TO REST	DEVELOPING YOUR STYLE & VOICE
CONSUMING ART	COLLABORATING WITH OTHERS
LETTING YOUR IMAGINATION WANDER	EXPANDING BEYOND YOUR COMFORT ZONE
ALIGNING WITH PURPOSE	SHOWING UP CONSISTENTLY
CULTIVATING YOUR ENERGY & CONSCIOUSNESS	LAUNCHING & SHARING YOUR WORK

SOMETIMES THE MOST
PRODUCTIVE THING
YOU CAN DO IS
NOTHING AT ALL

Chapter 2

SETTING AN INTENTION

A FEW YEARS ago, I took a flight from New York City to the Sacred Valley of Peru to attend an ayahuasca ceremony with an Amazonian shaman. I was more than a little nervous. When the plane landed in Peru, I had no idea what to expect. All I knew is that I felt stuck, both personally and professionally. My job in advertising had been driving me crazy. What once felt fun and exciting now felt serious and heavy. I needed a change in scenery, a new perspective. Now here I was in South America for the first time. After the plane landed, a car drove me several hours into the heart of Peru. I decided to let go of expectations and trust where the journey would take me.

The next evening, I sat in a humble wooden shelter with a small group of fellow travelers. The sun had set, and the room was illuminated by candlelight. The smell of burning palo santo and tobacco filled the room. Sitting on an altar—alongside small statues, beads, a picture of a jaguar, and other relics—was a glass container filled with dark-red liquid.

Ayahuasca is a psychoactive tea brewed from a unique combination of vines and leaves found in the Amazon. It has long been used by Indigenous South American tribes as a hallucinogenic medicine. Administered by a shaman, this brew is believed to give spiritual insights and heal energetic or emotional sickness that can manifest as physical ailments. In recent years ayahuasca has been known to help some people with psychological disorders such as addiction and PTSD. This medicine is not for everyone, and it should be taken with caution and respect. I did a lot of research before flying to Peru, but I still wasn't sure how I would react. Now, still disoriented from my strange, new surroundings, I was about to drink this powerful brew. *What have I gotten myself into?* I wondered.

The shaman sat quietly behind the altar wearing a colorful knitted hat and a long, white shawl. He was an older man, but his skin was youthful and glowing. The ambient hum of the jungle was the only noise until the shaman finally spoke.

"Before we begin, it's important to set an intention. Every thought is a prayer we send into the universe," he said. "The universe always responds to our prayers. Your intention is what you hope to learn or experience. It's not about controlling the journey. After all, the spirit of ayahuasca has a mind of her own. She will teach you whatever lesson you need to learn, but your intention helps to guide your journey. If you become lost or afraid, simply return your awareness back to your intention, back to your prayer."

I thought long and hard about my intention. Why had I come all the way to Peru to drink this strange medicine? What was I hoping to heal or learn? As usual, I had been feeling stressed and overworked back in New York. It felt like I was carrying heavy baggage. I wanted to let go but didn't know how.

"It is time." The shaman broke the silence. "Please come to the altar to receive your cup."

My intention, I finally decided, was to awaken a sense of childlike wonder inside myself, to stop taking my life and my career so seriously, and to remember how to play—to feel like an artist again, not just another cog in the corporate machine.

I whispered my intention to myself once, then twice, before walking to the altar to receive a cup of dark-red liquid, which I drank as quickly as possible. The taste was unbearable. As the medicine sank into my system, the shaman started singing. He shook a rattle and danced around the room as my perception of reality began to unravel.

Intentions, not expectations.

What is the purpose behind your creativity? All art serves a purpose. Every piece of writing or art transmits an energy that changes the world in some way, however big or small. Some art provides comfort. Some art is meant to shock and provoke. Some art inspires awe. Some art starts a dialogue that sparks social change. Some art shines a light on the dark corners of the human psyche that we'd rather ignore. As creatives, it's important to have a clear idea about the impact we want our work to make. Setting an intention gives us that clarity.

Your intention is the underlying purpose that motivates your action. This is more than just how you want your project to turn out. It's about the impact you want to make in the world.

When setting an intention, consider the following questions:

- Why do I feel compelled to create?

- What are my ultimate goals?

- What thoughts and emotions do I want to inspire in others?

- What impact do I want to make on society?

- How do I want this project to help me grow?

- What magic and medicine do I wish to offer the world?

Without a purposeful intention to fuel your work, it's easy to become frustrated or lost in the details. Having an intention helps you keep going when you'd rather quit. It's not about controlling the process. It's about guiding it forward, motivated by a purpose greater than yourself.

Intentions are different from expectations. Expectations are an attachment to specific results—an assumption about how things should and will turn out. Intentions, on the other hand, are about internal purpose and the impact we hope to achieve. In life and art, the end result is never fully in our control, but an intention is a North Star that helps us navigate the journey.

Example of an expectation: "I expect to write a bestselling book."

Example of an intention: "I intend to write about my own experiences with openness and vulnerability in order to help other people who are going through something similar."

With expectations, we become emotionally invested in a desired outcome that may never happen, which inevitably leads to disappointment. An intention, by contrast, is about the energy we put into the present moment and where we direct the antenna of our awareness. An expectation, being outwardly focused, is never in your control. An intention, being inwardly focused, is always in your control.

Expectations are the enemy of creativity. They bring unnecessary pressure and limit our creative potential. In my experience, the end result seldom resembles what I expected in the beginning. The work is shaped by the journey. Rather than anticipating a specific outcome, it's better to surrender control and leave space for the spirit of inspiration to flow through you. Give your creativity the freedom to become whatever it wants to be.

Think like a beginner.

There's a concept in Zen Buddhism called "beginner's mind." According to beginner's mind, too many preconceived ideas make our minds fixed and rigid. We get bogged down with information and old ways of doing things. The mind of a beginner, by contrast, is open and flexible.

Beginners are inspired because they see the world through a lens of curiosity and wonder.

It's best to approach life and art without preconceived ideas or expectations. According to the Zen monk Shunryū Suzuki, "If your mind is empty, it is always ready for anything, it is open to everything. In the beginner's mind there are many possibilities, but in the expert's mind there are few."

I still remember my first internship as an unpaid graphic designer. I showed up to the office with wide eyes and a wrinkled dress shirt. My mind was a blank slate—which is a nice way of saying I was clueless. But what I lacked in experience I made up for with curiosity. I wasn't afraid of asking stupid questions or suggesting stupid ideas. I learned fast because my mind was free from preconceived ideas about how things *should* be.

It's never too late to have beginner's mind. It's not about age; it's a mentality. Having beginner's mind is about asking questions and staying open minded, even when you *think* you already know the answer. It's about entertaining ideas that might sound weird at first. It's about seeing each challenge as a creative puzzle waiting to be solved.

The creative process is an act of perpetual discovery. Too much information leaves no space for inspiration. Creativity thrives when the mind is open to all possibilities.

How to set a creative intention.

Your intention should be about the impact you want to make in the world. It's not about achievements or details. Your intention should guide your overall vision while leaving plenty of freedom for the shape and texture to reveal themselves along the way. When we try to micromanage the process, we limit the magic of intuition and imagination to offer unexpected solutions.

An intention should be:

1. Thematic, not specific

Creating art is like landing a spaceship. First you want to steer your ship in the general direction of your planetary destination. Over time, the planet will come into view and you can adjust your velocity and directions accordingly. Start broad and gradually narrow your focus as you go.

2. Fluid and adaptable

You can have a single intention for all your work or you can revisit your intention from project to project. You can even change your intention in the middle of a project if a new direction reveals itself. The purpose of an intention isn't to limit. The purpose is to inspire. Be fluid and adaptable with your ideas, especially at the beginning.

3. Bigger than yourself

Shallow intentions produce shallow ideas. When our intentions are too self-centered—intending to become famous or to make a lot of money, for example—they probably won't inspire great ideas. Intentions are the well from which we draw the water of inspiration: the deeper the well, the more water we find. Besides, fame and money are natural outcomes from art that makes a deep connection with people, so focus on connection first.

Energy flows where attention goes.

Back in Peru, my ayahuasca ceremony was a voyage into the unknown depths of my subconscious mind. The shaman played a simple melody on his flute while portals to other worlds opened and faded in my mind, as though I were viewing reality from a hundred-thousand miles away.

At times I felt afraid. My ego was no longer in control. One minute I was flying and the next minute I was falling, and my heavy emotions were accelerating my descent. But I remembered what the shaman had told us: "If at any point you become lost or afraid, simply return your awareness back to your intention."

The creative process is similar to a psychedelic journey. Both are voyages into the unknown. We start without knowing exactly where we will end up. What happens along the way is anyone's guess. The journey isn't one of distance. It's a journey into the subconscious. There is no map or paved road to follow. The path is revealed step by step as we stumble forward in the dark. And we eventually reach an unexpected destination and learn many lessons along the way.

The final creative output never turns out exactly how we imagine. That's part of the magic. We can't fully control the process, but we can guide it. An intention is similar to a prayer. When we set an intention, we send a signal into the universe. You don't have to believe in a specific deity or higher power. Consciousness has a power unto itself. Energy flows where attention goes. Left to its own devices, the mind behaves like the rocky waves in an ocean storm, tossing our awareness in each and every direction. Intentions help guide us through the storm. "Paying" attention is "buying" reality. Invest your awareness wisely.

CREATIVE PLAYTIME

Find your why

In Simon Sinek's book *Start with Why*, he introduces a methodology for helping creatives, entrepreneurs, and leaders work with purpose and clarity. To find your "why," get out a notebook and write down answers for the questions below:

- *What* do I do? (the result) Example: I write poetry.

- *How* do I do it? (the process) Example: I take inspiration from the natural world.

- *Why* do I do it? (The purpose) Example: I want to inspire awe by bringing people's attention to beauty.

Your "why" is your intention. Think long and hard about your answer. Can you go even deeper? What is the reason behind the reason? Remember: the deeper your intention, the deeper your source of inspiration.

Write a billboard

Everything you say, do, and make is a message you are sending out into the world. The messages we send, whether subtle or overt, are like tiny seeds we are planting in the collective consciousness. Forget about your particular creative medium. What is the *message* that you want to go viral? Who are you? What do you stand for?

Imagine that you are given a giant billboard on a busy highway. Each year, millions of people will read your billboard. You can write anything you desire on the billboard. What is your message? Don't think of a commercial advertisement. Think of a message from your soul that you want to communicate. Write it down or type it on your computer or in a notes app on your phone. Save it and check it every few days to remind yourself of the message you want to put out into the world.

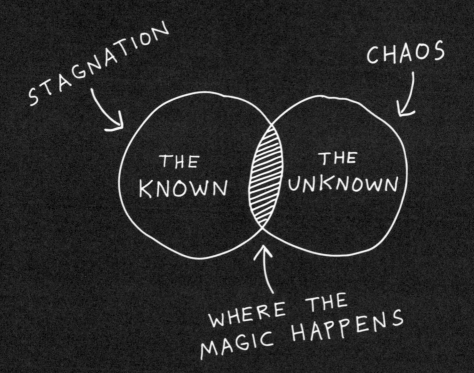

CREATIVITY IS A FLOWER

THE RAIN IS THE MUSE THAT SPARKS INSPIRATION.

THE SUNLIGHT IS THE TIME AND ATTENTION

YOU GIVE TO NURTURING YOUR IDEAS.

THE SOIL IS YOUR SUBCONSCIOUS MIND.

THE SEEDS ARE YOUR DAILY THOUGHTS AND HABITS.

THE CLIMATE IS THE MOOD AND VIBE YOU SET.

THE FLOWER IS YOUR CREATIVITY,

WHICH BLOOMS WITHOUT EFFORT

UNDER THE RIGHT CONDITIONS.

CHARLES BUKOWSKI

"DON'T TRY."

1920  1994

The poet Charles Bukowski has a simple epitaph engraved on his tombstone: "Don't try." This isn't a message about apathy. It's about giving up the need for egoic control and allowing life and art to unfold with minimal force or interference.

This is the difference between force and flow. While in flow, things happen without effort. Synchronicities emerge. A tree doesn't <u>try</u> to grow branches. A cloud doesn't <u>try</u> to rain. It is their nature, their dharma.

Instead of forcing, sink into your nature. Set down the need to control every detail and just let it happen. Like rain, like tears.

Chapter 3

GUIDES AND INSPIRATION

"If I have seen further than others, it is by
standing upon the shoulders of giants."

ISAAC NEWTON

BEFORE YOU CAN be a master, you must be a student. Having teachers and guides is the ultimate creative shortcut because we can learn valuable lessons without having to live through the trial and error of experience. Guides are those who are farther along the path than we are. It's not about copying their style—it's about learning the territory. Guides expand our awareness of what is possible.

Upon moving from Minnesota to New York City, I discovered Kundalini yoga. Combining postures with breath work, meditation, and mantra chanting, it was unlike any exercise I had done before, and it gave me a sense of inner peace to balance the external chaos of my new surroundings. During class, the instructors often spoke about a "golden thread" of teachers that stretches back into ancient history. The lineage of yoga, they said, reaches back thousands of years to the Vedic tradition in India, where students were taught the secrets of the body and mind from master teachers. From one teacher to the next to the next to the next, a golden thread connects us to the wisdom of the past.

No person is an island. Each teacher learned from those who came before, who in turn learned from those who came before. The golden thread also applies to creativity. Every artist and creator has been inspired by others, reaching back to our earliest songs, cave paintings, and creation myths.

Having guides and teachers is not in conflict with being original and innovative. Each creator bends and shapes the medium in their own unique way. Rules are meant to be broken. There is always new territory to discover. But your work will have more depth and stability when you are grounded in the roots of tradition.

We are what we consume.

Creative guides can appear in a number of forms. Maybe you're lucky enough to have a real-life mentor, perhaps a talented friend or a good professor. But more often than not, when it comes to creativity, we learn from consumption, by studying and absorbing the work of others. In this sense, the entire world is a university filled with art, writing, music, dance, and film to teach us the spectrum of creative expression.

If you want to make art, you need to consume art. Not just casually— *obsessively*. If you want to write books, you have to read books. If you want to make music, you have to listen to music. If you want to start a podcast, you have to listen to podcasts. If you want to make videos, you have to watch videos. If you want to be a public speaker, you have to listen to other public speakers. Absorbing the canon of art in your chosen medium will help you understand the territory so you can create with confidence and autonomy.

Guides pass on lessons that we can incorporate into our own work. The goal is to gather a toolkit of tips and tricks. Before Jack Kerouac wrote his famous novel *On the Road*, he typed out *The Great Gatsby* by F. Scott Fitzgerald in its entirety because he wanted to know how it would feel to type the words of a great novel. That's the power of guides. They help us understand and navigate our own creative journey.

You can also learn a lot by exploring art in other mediums and genres. I'm not a musician, but I obsessively listen to new music and eagerly await new albums from my favorite artists. Listening to new music keeps my finger on the pulse of culture and gives me inspiration to fuel my own creativity. It also helps with neuroplasticity, the mind's ability to change and adapt. As we age, our brains tend to form deep grooves based on habitual patterns. But when we actively seek out novelty, we form new neural pathways that help keep us young and inspired.

Part of the reward of consuming art is the joy of discovery. You never know what life-changing song, book, or movie might be waiting around the corner. That's why hip-hop music producers spend countless hours digging through old collections of vinyl records. Yesterday's forgotten soul song might provide the sample for tomorrow's number-one hit. You're only as original as the obscurity of your influences. Don't just skim the surface of popular art. Dive into the deep end to discover unexpected surprises.

It's also valuable to seek out influences from a diverse range of cultural perspectives. Much of the world's celebrated historical literature was written from a European or American male vantage point—a perspective that's not representative of the entire world. There are many cultural experiences worthy of exploration and celebration, including those from diverse nationalities, ethnicities, religions, genders, and sexualities. When we seek inspiration from multiple backgrounds, we become more well rounded and empathetic, both as humans and creators.

Poet and rapper Tupac Skakur opened my mind and heart when I discovered his music as a teenager. Although he was tragically killed by gunfire at age twenty-five, Shakur wrote songs that gave hope to a generation of young people living in urban communities overridden with gang warfare, drug abuse, poverty, and police brutality. Not only did he expose me to a new cultural perspective, he did so with a poetic honesty that was heartbreaking and beautiful.

Because of Tupac's formative influence on me as a teenager, I try to be socially conscious and inspire a better world in my own writing. Like the political anthems of John Lennon, Tupac's songs taught me the power of art as a catalyst for social change. His poetic use of language gave a relatable voice to a marginalized group of people. He also taught me that the best art tells the truth, even when—*especially* when—that truth is uncomfortable.

Consuming art is one way to get inspired. Another is to study the lives and ideas of your favorite creators. The ancient Vedic tradition that gave birth to yoga and Hinduism stressed the importance of a direct transmission of teachings from master to student. Finished art is the final packaged output: a beautiful and polished artifact. But it can be even more educational to go behind the scenes to understand the mindset of the creator. I highly recommend diving deep into the lives and perspectives of your favorite artists. Read biographies, listen to YouTube and podcast interviews, watch documentaries, and attend lectures, all of which are potent sources of creative transmission.

The world is your classroom.

Research is essential to creativity. This could mean studying the best creators in your field. It could mean researching a specific topic or historical period. Or it could simply mean keeping your eyes open and being perceptive in everyday life. There are stories and dramas unfolding all around us. When we pay attention, we tune into human nature, which gives us more fodder for creative thinking.

Think of the world like a classroom. No matter how old you are, there is always more to learn, more to absorb. Be a sponge for information and experiences. Seek out novelty. Study the people, places, and aesthetics that are related to your work.

You can rely on books, Wikipedia, and documentaries, but experience is the best teacher. If you want to create art, it's imperative to first live life—to travel, to witness, to feel, to fail, to be hurt, and to overcome. Whenever I break my routine and visit a novel location, my mind is always teeming with inspiration. Expand your horizons. Deepen your engagement with life. Study the world like a PhD student. Be a nerd for new discoveries. Your art will thank you.

Stealing fire.

In Greek mythology, the god Prometheus snuck into heaven so he could steal fire and bring it back to Earth. Being an artist is similar. We steal fire wherever we can find it. This isn't about copying someone else's work; it's about stealing techniques and inspiration that we can adapt to serve our own vision. We learn different lessons from different teachers. The beauty of art is that there are no borders. Unlimited styles and perspectives can coexist—each an ingredient to add to our own recipe.

Though it's useful to take inspiration from a variety of sources, it helps to have a few primary influences. This will give you a purposeful foundation, an understanding of your path and purpose in relation to all others. Every artist carries the torch of an ethos or aesthetic. We take the spirit handed down to us, adapt it for the times we live in, and pass it down again. The surface appearance looks different, but the spirit remains intact.

Before he dramatically reinvented jazz music, Miles Davis was a trumpet player in Charlie Parker's bebop band. He mastered this popular style before deconstructing the building blocks of jazz and putting them back together in new and exciting ways. Similarly, before John Coltrane began experimenting with bold, free-flowing melodies, he was a saxophone player in Miles Davis's band. Just as Miles learned from Parker, Coltrane learned from Miles. On the surface, each artist's music sounds different, but a golden thread of artistic spirit connects them, each building upon the lessons of the others.

The jazz lineage of Parker, Davis, and Coltrane was eventually passed down and integrated into hip-hop music. In the 1980s, the rapper Rakim was looking to expand the lyrical vocabulary and vocal cadence of the genre. Taking inspiration from John Coltrane, he studied how the saxophonist had created complex lyrical melodies with his horn, bopping from note to note in unexpected ways. Rakim incorporated this style into his vocal delivery, allowing him to stretch the art of rapping into uncharted territory. Rakim's lyrics and delivery would become the gold standard in hip-hop music for years to come.

Having guides and influences also applies to fields like science, technology, and engineering. Before he co-founded Apple, Steve Jobs was inspired by innovative scientists like Albert Einstein and Thomas Edison, but he also learned from original thinkers in other fields. When Apple released its famous "Think Different" ad campaign in 1997, Jobs featured many of his personal heroes, including the puppeteer Jim Henson, the pilot Amelia Earhart, and the movie director Orson Welles. It wasn't their specific work that inspired Jobs; it was their ability to innovate and think outside the box, proving that you can take inspiration from one field and apply it to another.

Finding my creative lineage.

I discovered my own creative lineage when I was seventeen. My friends were applying to college, and it was time to start thinking of which career I wanted to pursue. But none of the conventional options excited me. Deep down, I wanted to be a writer. But after speaking to my high school guidance counselor, none of the options she suggested (such as newspaper journalist or advertising copywriter) appealed to me. I wanted to make art, to write poetry. But it didn't seem like a realistic career path.

One day, while browsing a bookstore in Minnesota, I stumbled across a book of interviews with the poet Allen Ginsberg. I had never heard of Ginsberg before but the book looked interesting, so I bought it. Over the following week I devoured every word. It felt like a transmission from another dimension. There was something about Ginsberg's voice that felt like he was speaking directly to me. He was using art to tap into an organic spirituality that had nothing to do with organized religion. He saw humanity as inherently holy.

I later discovered that Ginsberg was influenced by the American poet Walt Whitman and the British poet and artist William Blake, both of whom used their creativity as a channel for mystical illumination. Ginsberg had a life-changing spiritual awakening in college when he experienced an auditory hallucination of William Blake reading his poem "Ah! Sun-flower" in his Columbia University dorm room. This revelation was followed by several days of mystical visions in which Ginsberg saw the presence of God in all things: the sky, the buildings, and the faces of his fellow students. He was forever changed and began using his own poetry as a canvas to allow the spontaneous life force of the universe to speak through him.

Ginsberg learned from Blake and Whitman, and in turn he transmitted this wisdom to a new generation of mystical poets and songwriters, including Bob Dylan and Patti Smith. In this tradition of writing that was both mystical and grounded in reality—finding the sacred in the profane—I discovered my spiritual and creative lineage. My seventeen-year-old self made a commitment to try—at least *try*—to follow the path of the illuminated artist and poet, no matter how long it would take, no matter how unrealistic it seemed at the time.

Many years later, after countless wrong turns, failures, and setbacks, I commemorated the release of my first published book by getting a tattoo of the word *Howl* in honor of Ginsberg's famous poem.

Find your creative lineage

Think back to the people who were influential on your creative journey. They could be a novelist, a musician, a poet, an artist, a spiritual guide, a teacher, or even a friend. Consider different types of guides. Who first inspired you to be creative? Who taught you the most about style and technique? Who helped to expand your cultural and artistic horizons? Who continues to push you to be better? Make a list of five to ten creative guides. Is there a common thread, either stylistically or philosophically, that ties them together? Now revisit their work with fresh eyes. Read their books. Listen to their music. Search YouTube and watch any talks or interviews available. See what you notice. What do you like? What don't you like? In a few sentences, write down what you learned from each guide.

Go on an inspiration scavenger hunt

If you want to feel more inspired, start consuming more art. Choose an author, a musician, or other type of artist you don't know much about. Take time to explore different genres or mediums. You can even dedicate one day a week to creative exploration. Read a book, listen to an album, visit a museum, or attend a lecture. Pay attention to what you find interesting. Write down what you learn. Borrow whatever you find inspiring.

Music meditation

Music is a great source of inspiration. It lifts our spirits and soothes the soul. Most people listen to music, but how often do they listen with full, uninterrupted attention? One of my favorite ways to connect with inspiration is to choose a great album, put on headphones, and listen to it from beginning to end.

For this exercise, choose a great album, perhaps one you've never heard before. (If you need a recommendation, you can research lists of the best albums ever, or by decade.) Listen at a time when you won't be disturbed. Pay attention to the lyrics, each instrument, and the way the album flows from song to song. Try this exercise with different artists and genres.

Some of my personal album recommendations include *Blood on the Tracks* by Bob Dylan, *Songs in the Key of Life* by Stevie Wonder, *Blue* by Joni Mitchell, *Norman Fucking Rockwell!* by Lana Del Rey, *Revolver* by The Beatles, *Kid A* by Radiohead, *Kind of Blue* by Miles Davis, *Survival* by Bob Marley and the Wailers, *Lifted* by Bright Eyes, *Low* by David Bowie, *Hissing Fauna, Are You the Destroyer?* by Of Montreal, *The Miseducation of Lauryn Hill* by Lauryn Hill, *The Velvet Underground & Nico* by The Velvet Underground and Nico, *1999* by Prince, and *Blonde* by Frank Ocean.

SAY YES TO ADVENTURE

BEFORE AN ARTIST CAN MAKE GOOD ART, THEY MUST GO OUT AND EXPERIENCE LIFE. BEFORE A WRITER CAN WRITE, THEY NEED SOMETHING TO WRITE ABOUT. IT'S NOT ENOUGH TO KNOW FACTS. YOU MUST KNOW FEELINGS – FEAR AND FORGIVENESS AND HATE AND SALVATION AND EVERYTHING IN BETWEEN.

SOME THINGS YOU CAN'T LEARN IN BOOKS OR PODCASTS OR DOCUMENTARIES. YOU HAVE TO WALK THROUGH THE FIRE AND BURN AWAY YOUR BIAS AND ILLUSIONS.

SAY YES TO THE ADVENTURE OF LIFE. FIND OUT WHAT YOU'RE CAPABLE OF. GET LOST. GO DANCING. LOOK THE DEVIL IN THE EYE. FALL IN LOVE. GET YOUR HEART BROKEN. MOVE TO A PLACE YOU'VE NEVER BEEN BEFORE. FEEL HAPPINESS SO DEEP IT MAKES YOU CRY. LEARN TO LAUGH AT YOUR SORROW.

AND ONCE YOU HAVE TRAVELED AND LEARNED AND LOVED AND LOST, GO BACK HOME AND MAKE YOUR ART. YOU WILL KNOW WHAT TO SAY, AND IT WILL BE TRUE.

HOW TO EXPAND:

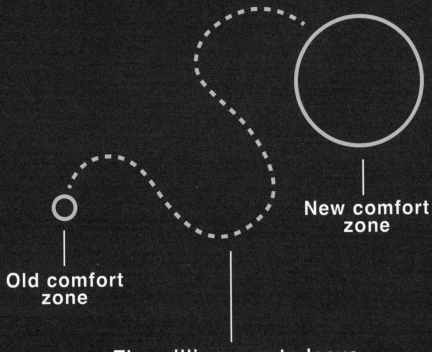

New comfort
zone

Old comfort
zone

The willingness to leave
behind old patterns and
beliefs to embark on a
meandering journey into
uncertainty and
self-discovery

Chapter 4

CULTIVATING INTUITION

WHEN PEOPLE TALK about abstract painters, a few names are usually mentioned first: Pablo Picasso, Wassily Kandinsky, Piet Mondrian, Jackson Pollock—men who revolutionized the art world in the first half of the twentieth century. What is rarely mentioned is that another relatively unknown artist began painting beautiful abstract canvases before any of them—as early as 1906. It turns out the father of abstract art isn't a father at all. She is a mother. And her name is Hilma af Klint.

Born in Sweden in 1862, Hilma af Klint was a precocious creative talent. She attended the Royal Academy of Fine Art in Stockholm, where she developed a signature style of dreamy realism. In 1880, when Hilma was eighteen years old, her sister died suddenly. Distraught and seeking solace, Hilma began a fascination with spirituality and the occult. She began attending seances where she practiced opening the channel of her consciousness to receive messages from unseen dimensions.

Hilma founded a collective of women known as De Fem (The Five). They met weekly to sit around an altar, pray, meditate, and conduct séances, claiming to receive messages from higher beings by entering a trance. It was during these seances that Hilma began receiving messages in the form of visual symbols. Setting aside conscious thought, she conjured abstract shapes and geometric patterns through automatic drawing. Little by little, a new mystical visual language began to emerge, as though Hilma was documenting images from the spirit world.

"The pictures were painted directly through me,

without any preliminary drawings, and with great force.

I had no idea what the paintings were

supposed to depict; nevertheless, I worked swiftly

and surely, without changing a single brush stroke."

HILMA AF KLINT

By the early 1900s—when Picasso was still in his Blue Period and Kandinsky was painting impressionistic landscapes—Hilma was channeling elaborate abstract paintings, rich with mystical symbolism. Hilma's creative process and her spiritual process were one and the same. Her direct and committed relationship with the muse inspired innovative, almost religious, symbolism beyond the reach of the logical mind.

Although Hilma lived to be eighty-one, she remained virtually unknown during her life. She believed the world was not prepared for the daring message and meaning of her work. Only a few of her paintings were displayed during her lifetime. She instructed her family to keep her work hidden until at least twenty years after her death. The decades passed, art movements rose and fell, and Hilma af Klint's entire body of work, including more than a thousand paintings and one hundred diaries, sat in storage—untouched and unseen, waiting to be discovered.

Where do ideas come from?

Where do ideas and inspiration come from? The truth is nobody knows the answer. One second there is no idea, then one suddenly appears like a light bulb turning on. It often feels like the process of idea generation happens outside our conscious control. It's not something we are doing; it's something that happens to us—*through* us. The original meaning of the word *inspiration* is to be guided by divine influence. The words *spirit* and *inspiration* can be traced back to the same Latin root: *spirare*, which means "breath."

Any act of creativity is breathing spirit into existence. That may sound strange. Exactly what "spirit" are we talking about? The ancient Greeks said it was the goddess spirit of the muse who delivered ideas like love letters to those open to receiving. Religious people might consider God to be the source of creative insight. Others might point to spirit guides, the higher self, ancestors, or even interdimensional beings. According to Carl Jung, there is a collective unconscious where all thoughts and ideas are waiting to be discovered.

Personally, I believe these are all metaphors for the same thing: *our own intuition*.

According to Hinduism, there is a spiritual world (Brahman) and a material world (Maya). Brahman is considered the true reality, an invisible dimension of pure energy, the fertile subconscious from which matter is born. The material world is called Maya, which is the temporary illusion of 3D reality, a shadow cast by the higher light of Brahman. Humans exist between these worlds. The body exists in Maya, but the soul's home is Brahman. Intuition is the bridge. When we tune in to our own inner voice, we connect with the frequency of Brahman, of source creation.

You can call the muse spirit whatever you like—or don't call it anything at all. The point isn't to give the muse a label. The point is to learn her language.

The language of intuition.

In modern society, we are taught the language of the mind. "I think, therefore I am," the philosopher René Descartes said. And such is the mantra of our times. We are trained to identify with our thoughts and perceive the world through the lens of reason and logic, but the nature of reality is more vast and mysterious than the human mind can comprehend with reason alone. We live in a multidimensional universe. The logical mind is an incredible tool for problem solving, but nature has an intelligence that surpasses our own, one that doesn't conform to our mental boxes and categorizations. The greatest scientists and philosophers cannot begin to explain where life truly comes from, how the design of the solar system came into being, what powerful energy is fueling the sun, or what happens to consciousness after the body dies.

There is only so much we can "figure out" conclusively. It's best to retain an open and curious mind. When our perception is too locked into a narrow or hyperrational state, value and meaning are reduced to mental abstractions. Purpose is replaced with productivity. Connection is replaced with profit. Open-minded curiosity is replaced with doubt and skepticism. When your only tool is a hammer, everything looks like a nail. And when your only tool is the intellect, everything looks like a problem that must be solved.

Creativity requires us to move from a state of alert problem-solving to a state of soft receptivity. From ego to intuition. Personally, my best ideas are seldom the result of overthinking or critical analysis. They pop into my head unexpectedly, like a revelation. It's not about solving a problem. It's about receiving an insight from beyond the conscious mind. I often look back on my writing and wonder where specific words and phrases came from. *These words didn't come **from** me*, I think. *They somehow came **through** me.*

Listening is just as important to the creative process as thinking—maybe more so. It's about slowing down the busy mind and becoming an antenna for the thought frequency of intuition.

Intuition can be hard to grasp because her language is quiet and soft, like a whisper. Attuning your awareness to the voice of intuition is like trying to catch a butterfly. It requires grace, not force. Patience, not strength.

The ego, by contrast, is our alert, reactive, problem-solving state of consciousness. It speaks like a barking dog, always on guard for threats. The role of the ego is to give us a sense of identity and to protect us from danger. There is nothing wrong with the ego. It is a valuable and necessary ally. But the process of generating ideas and inspiration requires a more delicate touch.

It took me a long time to learn to set my ego aside and trust my intuition. It helps to reassure the ego that it will get a chance to review, edit, and revise the work later on. It has a role, but the early stages of creativity are not the proper place for the ego's contribution. At the beginning, when ideas are not fully formed, it's best to withhold criticism and judgment. Give yourself space to listen, and give your ideas room to grow without pressure or expectation.

How to catch bigger fish.

Creativity is similar to fishing. Your mind is the water, and ideas are the fish. Listening to your ego is like fishing in a shallow pond. You're only skimming the surface of your mind's potential. Meanwhile, the subconscious mind is a vast and mysterious ocean. Quieting your busy ego and listening to your intuition is like fishing in a deep ocean. You have access to much more rich and exotic ideas and insights.

"Ideas are like fish," said film director David Lynch. "If you want to catch little fish, you can stay in the shallow water. But if you want to catch the big fish, you've got to go deeper. Down deep, the fish are more powerful and more pure. They're huge and abstract. And they're very beautiful."

During my advertising career in New York City, my mind was fishing in the shallow water of ideas. I was productive—extremely so. Our team was cranking out logos, websites, and marketing campaigns at breakneck speed, but my productivity wasn't connected to intuition. There were too many distractions, too many urgent deadlines. It was like working for a creative fire department. Each day, each meeting, there was another emergency to deal with. My awareness was hyperfocused, and my ego was running on overdrive.

> "The mind rebels against the unknown, so it moves from the known to the known, from habit to habit, from pattern to pattern. Such a mind never abandons the known to discover the unknown."
>
> JIDDU KRISHNAMURTI

My lifestyle didn't help either. I was drinking too much coffee and alcohol, eating junk food, and not meditating or exercising enough. My information diet was just as bad. I was watching television filled with mindless advertising and sensationalized news. My awareness was held captive by the commercialized surface reality around me. I wasn't diving into the deep water of my subconscious, and therefore I wasn't catching any big fish.

It didn't happen overnight, but I gradually learned to move my awareness away from my ego and toward my body and intuition. This change in awareness required a change in lifestyle. Everything we consume—from food to chemicals to music to media—affects our consciousness. The more I cleaned up my lifestyle, the more my awareness expanded.

I realized that my busy mind was not my only navigational tool. The energy of the body holds an innate, subtle intelligence that is beyond the conscious mind. Certain things cannot be known by thinking; they can only be known by feeling. Creativity is not a problem to solve. It is a message that we receive through awareness and transmit through expression. The deeper the awareness, the deeper the messages we receive.

The highest calling requires the deepest grounding. The tallest trees have the strongest roots. Your dreams don't start in the sky. They start in the deep, dark soil. These days, when I sit down to write, I start by scanning my body to see how I feel. What emotions do I notice? What sort of energy is moving through the world? What lesson is the universe trying to teach me? This practice is similar to meditation, and it opens my awareness to hear the voice of the muse, which is my own intuition.

Cultivating healthy mental soil.

Think of your subconscious mind as the soil in a garden. The quality of the soil determines what grows. If your mind's soil is full of poison—the chemicals from junk food, the clutter of worry and overthinking, the mental static from gossip and bad TV—the flowers of your ideas won't be healthy.

Preparing the soil of your subconscious to be a clear channel for intuition and inspiration is a lifelong pursuit. Just like a farmer must consistently tend to his soil, we must consistently tend to our minds. Following are some important areas of consideration when cultivating your intuition:

1. **Diet.** The food we eat has a huge effect on our consciousness. Having a clean, light diet helps the mind stay open and active. I recommend sticking to the essentials. Avoid sugar, excessive snacking, and processed foods. Intermittent fasting is also a good way to notice the relationship between diet and consciousness.

2. **Media.** We are what we consume. Just as some food is toxic and unhealthy, some media is toxic and unhealthy. My intuition improved greatly when I stopped trying to keep up with every news story. Limit the time you spend on media, including

social media, and do your best to seek out quality and reliable sources. And give yourself occasional breaks. Just as intermittent fasting is good for the body, intermittent media fasting is good for the mind.

3. **People.** We are greatly affected by the people we spend time with. It's been said that each person becomes the average of the five people with whom they spend the most time. It's important to surround yourself with people who uplift and inspire you. This includes those you follow on social media. Your energy and attention are sacred. Don't give them away to people who drag you down.

4. **Environment.** The space around us impacts the space inside us. A messy house leads to a messy mind. Cleaning your home can kickstart a cleaner consciousness. Treat your creative area like a sacred space. It also helps to add variety and to spend time in new spaces, especially in nature. Being in nature helps to restore our energy and renew the mind.

5. **Chemicals.** All chemicals affect consciousness differently. Some, like caffeine or alcohol, may narrow our focus. Others, like psychedelics, expand our awareness. There are no good or bad chemicals. It's about using the right chemicals in the right amount for the right purpose. It's a good idea to pay attention to the chemicals you consume and observe how they impact your physical and mental well-being.

6. **Movement.** Nothing gets the creative juices flowing faster than moving the body. I used to spend long hours hunched over my computer screen, never taking a break to stretch or exercise. I thought I was too busy to move my body, but my energy quickly evaporated and I was working on fumes.

YIN: CREATIVE BEING

Physical movement ignites our energy so we can tap into more inspiration. Try dancing around the room, shaking your limbs, going for a run, or doing some yoga poses. You won't regret it.

7. **Inspiration.** Creative people need to consume creativity on a regular basis. It keeps us inspired and opens us to new perspectives. Visit an art museum, go to a concert, read a new book, watch a highly rated movie, see a comedy show. Don't limit yourself to one medium or style. Explore beyond the familiar.

8. **Mindfulness.** Still water is the most clear. The same is true of the mind. When our thoughts are racing in multiple directions, it's like waves crashing on the ocean surface. Having a mindfulness practice such as meditation helps us calm the crashing waves so we can see and think clearly. Meditation is one of the oldest and most reliable tools for cultivating healthy mental soil. The goal of meditation is not to stop thinking. The goal is to become the observer of your thoughts rather than blindly reacting to them.

Your mind is a sanctuary.

It has been calculated that the average human has more than fifty thousand thoughts every single day, but most of these are mental clutter. When it comes to creativity, more thinking is not always better. Intuition is natural. It isn't something that needs to be learned or forced. Rather, it is our effortless state of consciousness when we strip away the mental clutter and social conditioning that distract us from our inner wisdom.

The muse is quiet and sensitive, like a bluebird prancing across the morning grass. She is easily startled by too much activity. Don't try to capture her. She will only run away. It's not about forcing ideas. It's about attracting them. Cultivate stillness inside yourself. Make your mind a sanctuary where the muse feels safe to visit.

Hilma and the spiral temple.

When Hilma af Klint began making abstract paintings, she received a channeled message during a séance. The message instructed her to prepare a collection of work to be displayed inside a spiral temple. Hilma had no idea what or where this temple was, but she dutifully took the assignment to heart, composing a collection of mystical paintings to one day hang inside a spiral temple. After Hilma passed away in 1944, her collection, which she called "paintings for the temple," went into a long period of hibernation. Decades passed. The world changed. And the name Hilma af Klint remained unknown.

In 2018, while living in Manhattan, I was scrolling Instagram when I noticed a new art exhibit at the Guggenheim Museum. The paintings were bright, alive, vibrant, new. I didn't recognize the name of the artist. Assuming she was a fresh face on the art scene, I searched Instagram for her profile, hoping to learn more about this budding new talent. No profile was found. In fact, the artist had been dead for sixty-nine years. It was Hilma af Klint.

The next day, I attended the exhibit. It was my first time visiting the Guggenheim, a historic building designed by architect Frank Lloyd Wright, which opened in 1959. It was unlike any building I had seen before. The entire circular structure was designed as a winding spiral. The stark white interior and exterior resembled a modern temple. And as I ascended the winding walkway and marveled at the beautiful paintings, I realized that this was it—Hilma's spiral temple—displaying the work she had prepared specifically for this occasion.

"Hilma af Klint: Paintings for the Future," the name of the Guggenheim exhibit, was a roaring success, attended by more than six-hundred thousand people. It was the most visited show ever in the museum's history. And the story of art would never be the same.

Open your channel

Evaluate your daily habits and determine where your consciousness is being harmfully influenced (diet, media intake,
etc.). Make a list so you know the things you need to start
cutting back on or eliminating. Next, begin a daily mindfulness practice. This can be as simple as taking two minutes
each day to practice deep breathing. Going for a walk,
meditating, and even sunbathing are all activities that foster
mental wellness. Make them your new habits.

Make an artist altar

Making the room where you create a sacred space will
help you get into the right mindset and summon the spirit
of the muse. Choose an area to designate as your altar. It
could be a shelf, a small table, or another surface area. Fill
the space with artifacts that inspire you, such as crystals,
statues, candles, pictures, or incense. Include a mix of spiritual and creative inspiration. For example, include photos,
books, albums, or other souvenirs to represent your favorite artists. Artistic iconography can be just as powerful as
spiritual iconography. Keep this space clean and organized,
a symbol of your dedication to your craft.

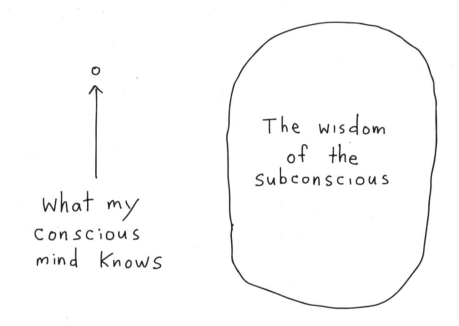

o

↑

what my
conscious
mind knows

The wisdom
of the
subconscious

INTUITION IS THE BRIDGE

The muse is a generous lover.

But she is also shy,

and needs you to make the first move.

Show up consistently,

with reverence and open ears,

free of your own agenda.

She needs to know that you are reliable,

a trustworthy keeper of her secrets.

"CREATIVITY IS SPIRITUAL"

THE BREATH IS THE DIVINE ESSENCE OF SOURCE CREATION

1

2

THE INSTRUMENT IS THE ARTIST, A THREE-DIMENSIONAL HUMAN CHANNEL

3

THE MUSIC IS THE EXPRESSION, A CO-CREATION BETWEEN HEAVEN AND EARTH

Chapter 5

CREATIVITY AND EMOTION: A LOVE STORY

"A work of art which did not begin
in emotion is not art."

PAUL CÉZANNE

EMOTION IS THE underlying energy that fuels creativity. Before we can make something, we must have an idea. And before we can have an idea, we must have a feeling. Feeling comes before thought. Therefore, listening to and processing our emotions are essential parts of the creative process.

Like a deep exhale, art offers a cathartic release, both to the creator and the receiver. It can inspire awe, curiosity, hope, love, and excitement. Or it is an empathetic medicine that soothes our pain. Emotions are invisible and often hard to define, but art helps us to navigate and understand the inner world of felt sensation.

The creative process is a safe space to explore and express all emotions. No feeling is taboo. No pain or vulnerability is too naked. It's about being honest with yourself and paying attention to what your body is telling you, then using your art to give form to the emotion, setting it free from the body's memory.

All emotions are valid.

Art exists within every facet of society. Happy people make art. So do sad people. Human creativity can be used to express a wide range of emotions and ideas, from the sacred to the profane and everything in between. Art can shock and provoke. It can inspire awe and wonder. It can fuel anger that sparks social change. It can make us cry tears of sadness and joy.

The paintings of Vincent van Gogh express an intense pathos and moody melancholy. The literature of Franz Kafka elicits a sense of dark introspection and paranoia. The music of The Beatles inspires feelings of love and universal connection. The speeches of Malcolm X express sacred rage toward social injustice. The writing of Sylvia Plath portrays a good-natured woman struggling with isolation and depression. All types of art—just like all emotions—are valid because they are honest reflections of the creator's personal experience.

When we feel sad, there is comfort in listening to sad music because it reminds us that we are not alone. It's okay to feel how we feel. In fact, it is essential to our well-being to allow ourselves to feel our feelings without resistance or bypassing. Feeling emotions is how we process them. When we fail to feel or process our emotions, they fester beneath the surface and emerge in unexpected forms such as hate or resentment, or they will decay into sickness. We must feel in order to heal.

The full spectrum of emotions.

In his book *Power vs. Force*, David R. Hawkins charted the spectrum of human emotion from the highest frequency (most expansive) to the lowest frequency (most contracted). Here are Hawkins's conclusions:

1. Enlightenment
2. Peace
3. Joy
4. Love
5. Reason
6. Acceptance
7. Willingness
8. Neutrality
9. Courage
10. Pride
11. Anger
12. Desire
13. Fear
14. Grief
15. Apathy
16. Guilt
17. Shame

We all aspire to be toward the top of this list, and I believe this is achievable for every human being. But sometimes life has other plans. We can't always choose our environments, especially when we are young. Many of us are born into situations that inflict deep trauma on the psyche and heart. Therefore, if we find ourselves in a state of anger, shame, or fear, it is not indicative of a character flaw. It is a response to our environment. All emotions are valid and have something to teach us.

For example, anger may be perceived as a "negative" emotion, but for someone living in a state of shame or apathy, anger is a way to reclaim the power they have lost. The punk-rock music from the late 1970s used anger as a tool to escape apathy and express frustration toward social conformity and government corruption. Similarly, hip-hop music is often criticized as a shallow celebration of wealth and material excess. This criticism fails to account for the impoverished background of many of the artists. When someone is coming from a place of desire or anger, pride is a positive step toward self-worth and personal sovereignty.

It's best not to wallow in contracting, low vibrational emotions. But on the journey to self-actualization, both as humans and creators, we need to be honest about our feelings. We can't automatically jump from shame to joy, bypassing all the steps in between. Our emotions must be felt and processed before we can advance to the next stage. Art is an outlet to feel, understand, express, and transmute these emotions.

Creativity as a healing modality.

In the middle of 2020, Los Angeles was in a state of emergency. Citywide lockdowns from the COVID-19 pandemic had led to vacant streets and bankrupt businesses. Black Lives Matter protests following the tragic death of George Floyd had devastated the city. The buildings on Abbot Kinney Boulevard were boarded up to protect them from looters. The National Guard was deployed. Military vehicles and soldiers with machine guns were stationed along Hollywood Boulevard. Economic depression had accelerated the already prevalent homelessness crisis, and communities of tents had taken over the sidewalks near Venice Boardwalk. To make matters worse, it was fire season. The sky across the entire West Coast was tinted orange from smoke. More than once we were forced to evacuate our home in Topanga Canyon because of looming wildfire threats.

Such was the state of the city when my partner and I decided to leave Los Angeles and move to Austin, Texas. The choice of Austin was arbitrary— neither of us had ever been to the city before. We didn't have any friends there. Yet intuition told us the move was the right decision. Ready for a new adventure, we packed our bags, said goodbye to Los Angeles, and drove 1,300 miles through the western desert to our new Texas home.

Austin, we learned, has long been a hub for creative expression. For decades, misfit artists and musicians have traveled across the country to call the city home. "Keep Austin weird" is the city's motto. The welcoming, open-minded nature of the community encourages honest, authentic expression, as exemplified by local artists like Janis Joplin and Daniel Johnston. It's been said that a nearby landmark called Enchanted Rock—considered a sacred site by the Indigenous Comanche people—is an energy center that helps to heal and unlock the throat chakra, allowing people to express themselves more fully and clearly.

Perhaps no artist better represents the spirit of Austin than country singer Willie Nelson. After spending many years in Nashville as a clean-cut professional songwriter, Willie had achieved modest success writing songs for others, but he failed to break through as a solo performer. The Nashville sound was too polished, too pretty. It was an awkward fit for Willie, a rough-around-the-edges Texas native. He wore a big smile on his clean-shaven face, but under the surface his soul was suffocating.

Finally, he couldn't take it anymore. Willie left Nashville and bought a horse ranch in Texas, where he began performing at small honky-tonk bars in Austin. Free from the commercial restraints of Nashville, he could finally express himself fully. He grew a beard and ponytail, wrapped a bandana around his head, and started smoking copious amounts of cannabis. He developed his own unique style of music that infused country, pop, blues, and jazz. It sounded nothing like the polished Nashville sound. Crowds loved it. This new style came to be known as "outlaw country." Willie Nelson, against all odds, became one of the most successful and beloved country music artists of all time.

• • •

Shortly after we arrived in Austin, the COVID-19 restrictions in Texas began to lift. Businesses reopened and crowds were allowed to gather in public. After nearly a year in quarantine, it was a much-needed exhale. I was ready to stop interacting with people exclusively through computer screens and make some real human connections in my new community.

I launched a monthly open-mic night and creativity gathering called Sunflower Club. The idea behind the name is that sunflowers will twist their faces toward sunlight in order to feel the light and warmth. Artists, I believe, do this too. We turn our faces toward the light, toward beauty, toward art wherever we can find it. The sunflower is, in my opinion, a symbol for art and creativity of all kinds.

> "Poetry is the one place where people can speak their original human mind. It is the outlet for people to say in public what is known in private."

ALLEN GINSBERG

Each month our club gathered to express ourselves in the form of poetry, storytelling, and song. Men and women of all ages—many who had never performed in public before—expressed their most intimate thoughts and feelings: a confessional about cheating on a husband, the feeling of depression and isolation during quarantine, a song sung as a love letter to someone's younger self. One woman recited a poem written by her high school boyfriend before he committed suicide twenty years earlier.

After a year of lockdown, it was like the floodgates had opened and our emotions could flow again. We listened together, laughed together, and cried together. It was refreshing and cathartic, both for the performers and the audience. I realized that nearly everyone I know is a writer in their private life, recording reflections in notebooks that perhaps nobody will ever read. Being given a forum to express our creativity in public—to be seen and heard without judgment—was an experience of emotional healing.

(Since launching, Sunflower Club has grown into a global decentralized creative community, with branches sprouting up all over the world. Sunflower Club is an open forum for people to express their innate creativity. All modes of expression are welcome, from poetry to music to dance to storytelling. If you're interested in hosting a Sunflower Club in your community, visit jamesmccrae.com to learn how.)

One of the first friends I made in Austin was a poet and singer named Emma Zeck, who taught me much about creativity as a modality for processing emotion and healing trauma. Like so many people, Emma grew up in a tumultuous environment where it was unsafe to speak openly and express herself. The pains we experience in childhood, when not properly processed, tend to be suppressed deep within the body, leading to emotional and physical complications. Healing our unresolved trauma is important to our well-being, both as individuals and a society.

Through her poems and songs, Emma uses creativity to explore and release her deepest emotions, including pain, heartbreak, joy, lust, worship, and self-love. No topic or feeling is off limits. Listening to Emma perform is like watching a bird escape its cage and fly toward the sun, finally liberated.

Because we are friends, I usually know what Emma is going through, whether it's falling in love, a breakup, or a period of quiet reflection. And when I see her perform, it's all there, laid out naked for the world to see. Her expression is cathartic, both for Emma and the audience. And her courageous vulnerability gives others permission to excavate and release their own emotions—both the good and the bad—through art.

Sensitivity is a superpower.

Around the turn of the twentieth century, coal miners brought caged canaries into work sites. The mines emitted dangerous gases, including carbon monoxide. The canary would be affected by the gas before the humans.

If the canary died, the miners knew it was time to leave. The canary served as an early warning.

Creatives are the canaries in the coal mine of society. No, we don't die from dangerous gases, but creative people, being sensitive by nature, feel things before others. The changing mood of the collective is first picked up by the artist's antenna and communicated through creative expression.

In 1964, when Bob Dylan released his prophetic anthem, "The Times They Are a-Changin'," he was ringing a bell to alert the world of the massive cultural shifts that would soon take place. He could see these changes coming because he had already felt them inside himself.

The fiction of Octavia E. Butler was also visionary. In her 1993 novel *Parable of the Sower*, she portrays the post-apocalyptic aftermath of a global pandemic, which alters the fabric of society. The deep feelings of isolation and uncertainty felt altogether too real and immediate as I read the book during the 2020 pandemic. Butler possessed an attuned emotional awareness that allowed her to tap into the collective mood thirty years in the future.

Artists have many important social roles. We provide beauty, entertainment, inspiration, education, and spiritual insight. One overlooked role is that of visionary and prophet. Being a prophet does not necessarily mean knowing the future. It means knowing yourself and your own emotions. On some level, we are all connected. The winds that blow through society touch us all. When we tune into our own emotions, we also tune into the changing winds of culture. Sensitivity is a superpower. The deeper we feel inside ourselves, the further we see outside ourselves.

Transmuting emotion into art.

The mind and body are not in opposition. They are intimately connected. In fact, our emotions are often the unseen motivating force behind our thoughts. We think something because we feel it first. As such, it's important for creatives to be in touch with our bodies and feelings. Creativity that is informed by emotional sensitivity will be richer, deeper, and more relatable than creativity guided by intelligence alone. Emotion is the glue that binds us together as humans.

Depending on our life experiences, different people will have different thoughts, but the common language of fear, heartbreak, anger, love, hope, and joy is shared by all. When we tap into our emotions to fuel our art, we are tapping into the collective emotional body. If I am feeling a certain way, there's a good chance that millions of others are feeling something similar. Our reasons may be different, but the feeling connects us.

I have traveled all around the world, but the most important journey I have ever taken—both as a human and an artist—is the eighteen inches between my head and my heart. The body has an intelligence that surpasses the intelligence of the mind. Much of what we *think*, whether we realize it or not, is based on how we *feel*. Being in touch with our body and emotions gives us a deeper understanding of ourselves and the world around us.

My creative process often begins with me sitting down in a comfortable position and checking in with my body. *How am I feeling? What are my emotions trying to tell me? If I'm feeling angry, where is that showing up in my body? Is my chest tight? Is my stomach clenched?* When we are guided by emotions instead of only thought, we are closer to the source of creative energy. The ideas we generate will be more clear and impactful because they're rooted in the body's intelligence.

Creative expression is a healing modality. Like therapy, it moves emotional energy into the mind's awareness so it can be released by the body. Emotions are not only valid, they are essential. They contain wisdom and intelligence in the form of felt presence. Pay attention to your body. Listen to your feelings. Take your pain, your sadness, your hope, your love, your loneliness, your existential dread, and transmute them into art.

Draw your emotions

Grab a notebook or piece of paper. Sit down in a comfortable position. Bring your awareness into your body. Notice how you feel. Are you happy? Sad? Tired? Don't judge your emotions. Simply notice them. Now draw a representation of how you feel. Don't think too much about it. Let your emotions guide you. Your drawing can be messy, simple, abstract, or figurative. You can even add words if you feel like it. It doesn't matter. The point is to process your emotions by getting them out of your body and onto the page.

Express your voice out loud

Making art in private is healing unto itself, but it's even more cathartic to express yourself out loud, especially in public. For this exercise, write a poem, journal entry, or short story that reveals something personal. Show some blood. Don't try to project an image of polished perfection. Take your mask off. Let us see your scars.

Next, read your piece out loud. You can simply recite it to yourself in front of a mirror. Or you can find a friend or group of friends to read to. You can even initiate a sharing circle that gives your friends a forum to express too. Or you can find an open-mic night in your town and share your piece publicly. The important thing is to let your vocal cords discharge whatever emotion you're holding within.

MAKING ART
IS LIKE MAKING LOVE

1. Vulnerability is key.
   You have to be naked.

2. Overthinking kills the magic.

3. There's no wrong way to do it.
   It's about personal preference
   and playful experimentation.

4. You can keep it to yourself
   but it's more fun to share
   with others.

5. There's a time to go slow
   and a time to go fast. Follow
   where the energy takes you.

6. You can't force it. The
   muse demands patience
   and delicate seduction.

7. It's a sacred ritual that
   gives birth to new creation.

WHAT PEOPLE SEE VS. THE REALITY

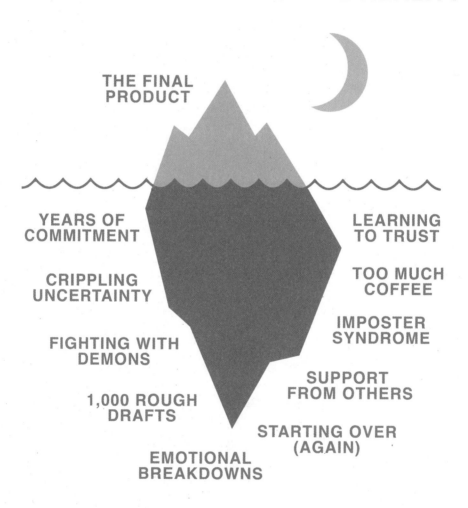

THE FINAL
PRODUCT

YEARS OF
COMMITMENT

LEARNING
TO TRUST

CRIPPLING
UNCERTAINTY

TOO MUCH
COFFEE

IMPOSTER
SYNDROME

FIGHTING WITH
DEMONS

SUPPORT
FROM OTHERS

1,000 ROUGH
DRAFTS

STARTING OVER
(AGAIN)

EMOTIONAL
BREAKDOWNS

Chapter 6

IMAGINATION: SEEING WITH YOUR THIRD EYE

"We live in condensations of our imagination."

TERENCE MCKENNA

EVER SINCE MY childhood I dreamt of living in New York City. There was a magnetic pull that I couldn't explain. It probably had something to do with so many of my favorite writers and artists having lived there. Walt Whitman, Edgar Allan Poe, Andy Warhol, Henry Miller, Billie Holiday, Bob Dylan, Joan Didion, Allen Ginsberg, Jean-Michel Basquiat, Patti Smith—the list goes on and on. But growing up in a small town on the Minnesota prairie, New York City might as well have been Jupiter. It didn't seem realistic. I had traveled no farther than South Dakota or Wisconsin. Nonetheless, I held the idea in the back of my mind, daydreaming of being an artist in the Big Apple, and maybe even writing books.

After graduating from art school in Minneapolis, I began a career in advertising as a graphic designer, spending long hours sitting in front of a computer designing logos, websites, and advertisements. Working in a professional office was new to me. It was a big adjustment getting used to client demands and tight deadlines. Overall, it was a good career. I was being paid to be creative, but deep down I couldn't shake the desire to move to New York City and write books. Yet it still didn't seem possible. I didn't even know where to start.

The universe works in mysterious ways. Sometimes a step forward looks like a step back. Without warning, I was fired from my job. My life was thrown upside down as I tried to figure out what to do next. Meanwhile, New York City kept trickling into my imagination like a leaky water faucet I couldn't turn off. *Drip, drip, drip, drip.* Finally, I couldn't ignore it any longer. It was now or never. Even though I didn't have a plan or much money, I decided to sell my possessions, say goodbye to friends and family, and buy a one-way ticket from Minneapolis–Saint Paul International Airport to LaGuardia in New York City.

It wasn't an easy transition. Having spent most of my life on the snowy Minnesota prairie, I had a hard time finding my place in the demanding, fast-paced culture of Manhattan. I had wanted to write books, but I couldn't even find a job. And the little money I had saved was dwindling.

Just when I was starting to lose hope, the unimaginable happened. It was a late night in October when Hurricane Sandy came storming into the Eastern Seaboard and walloped the city like a surprise punch in the face. It was the largest storm ever recorded in New York City. I had just started renting an apartment at the bottom of Queens, on Jamaica Bay. By midnight the floor was three feet under water. The apartment was destroyed; I was homeless.

Needless to say, my move to New York City wasn't exactly turning out as I had hoped. I didn't have a job, a place to live, or much money left. *Thanks for nothing*, I told my imagination. I was convinced that I had made a terrible mistake.

My options were limited. So, when my friend Jake, who had also been displaced by the hurricane, called and told me he had access to a small cottage on a remote Caribbean island. I said yes without hesitation. The next thing I knew, I was sitting alone on the white sand of Flamenco Beach on the island of Culebra, gazing into the Atlantic Ocean. My mind was running a million miles a minute. Left alone with my thoughts, my deepest fears and insecurities rose to the surface. *Now what?* I thought. I felt like a complete failure.

Culebra is a small, sparsely inhabited island. There was nowhere to go and nothing to do, so I sat on the sand for hours on end and watched the steady ebb and flow of the ocean tide, like a prolonged state of meditation. *Inhale. Exhale. Tide in. Tide out. Inhale. Exhale. Tide in. Tide out.*

Eventually my nervous system started to calm and my mind began to relax. All of these negative thoughts and insecurities, I realized, were just projections from my ego. Just because my mind told me something didn't make it true. This was a liberating realization. I am not my thoughts. And I am not my failures. I am not my ego.

In my newfound stillness I noticed another, quieter voice. It wasn't so much inside my head as it was a feeling inside my body. This voice, I realized, was my intuition. And I suddenly realized that these two voices—my ego and my intuition—are always speaking to me, competing for my attention. My ego caused me to overthink and worry. My intuition caused me to relax and trust the unfolding of my life.

Suddenly a book idea popped into my head. It was a book about ego and intuition—and learning the difference between the two. In an instant, I knew that I would write and publish this book, and it would be called *Sh#t Your Ego Says*. I didn't yet know how, but I could see it all in my mind. I could visualize the book cover and feel the texture of the pages. And I realized that my imagination didn't lead me here, to this remote island, by mistake. I was here to learn the lessons I needed to write the book. What appeared to be a huge crisis was actually a major opportunity.

So, I sat on the white sand of Flamenco Beach, closed my eyes, and held the idea in my imagination. I held it in my imagination. I held it in my imagination.

Imagination comes before reality.

Every single thing that humans have created on Earth—from great works of art to technology to businesses to political systems to romantic relationships—began as a tiny seed of imagination. Like childbirth, the art of bringing ideas to life begins with conception. Anything that is born must first be conceived, held, and nurtured in the mind.

We often think of imagination as a passive act. Our dreams are just that—dreams. But the deeper truth is that all creation begins as a dream. Thoughts become things. Consciousness carries an energetic frequency that interacts with the material world. Nothing can grow in the physical world until it has first been planted, nurtured, and developed in the mind. We cannot fight against the way things are. We must conceive and create something better.

Imagination is the best weapon in the war against reality.

According to the Greek philosopher Plato, there is a world of ideas—"Platonic ideals"—that is more real than the world of physical objects. The material world is a shadow cast by this world of pure thought. The ancient Vedic tradition suggests a similar idea: the universe is composed of two worlds: Brahman and Maya. Brahman is the eternal world of spirit and energy. Maya is the temporary illusion of time, space, and matter. Humanity originates from Brahman and temporarily inhabits the material world of Maya. Rituals such as prayer, meditation, and chanting are ways to access Brahman while residing in the physical dimension. This is not so different from the creative process. Our imagination reaches beyond the limitations of time and space to bring back messages from somewhere else.

Imagination is also a form of extrasensory perception. This is your third eye, your ability to perceive and nurture ideas in your mind, your sandbox for the reality you wish to create. It's almost like being able to see in the dark. The role of humans, especially artists, is to explore this unmapped world of ideas and bring back relics in the form of creative output. This is the alchemical process of manifesting the unseen into the physical realm. Imagination is the vision that enables us to navigate the terrain.

Even great scientific discoveries start in the imagination. Albert Einstein's famous theory of relativity, which ushered in a new understanding of reality, didn't begin with lab experiments or complicated math equations. Einstein was a dreamer. His preferred method of scientific exploration was to sit quietly and ponder the universe. For him, science began in the imagination.

Einstein came up with the theory of relativity while leisurely sitting on a bench watching trains pass. He imagined two bolts of lighting hitting a passing train at the exact same moment, one at the front of the train, the other in the back. From his vantage point as an observer, the light from each bolt would reach him at the same time, therefore the lightning strikes would appear to be simultaneous. He also theorized that a passenger on the train would experience the lightning bolt at the front of the train striking before the lightning bolt at the back of the train. Both perspectives—the passenger on the train and the observer on the platform—are correct according to each frame of reference. This story, conjured in Einstein's imagination, unlocked an insight about the relationship between speed and time that would change our understanding of reality. The math came later.

Widening your perception.

Some people are born with, or learn to develop, perception beyond the five senses. These people often find roles in society such as spiritual guides, psychics, shamans, or energy healers. But that heightened perception could also be as simple as having a strong intuition. Most people are familiar with the sensation of having a "feeling" about something—an instinct—without tangible evidence. This is a special form of perception.

We tend to think that our five senses represent the full scope of reality. What we can see, hear, taste, smell, and touch is all there is. But in truth, our senses conceal more information than they reveal. For example, look at the electromagnetic light spectrum. The portion of light that can be perceived by the human eye is surprisingly small. Similarly, there are entire ranges of sound frequency beyond our ability to hear. Perceiving with the five senses is like living inside a large house with only a single, narrow window. There is much more happening beyond our scope of perception.

This begs the question: How can we widen the scope of perception beyond the limits of the five senses? This is the mysterious realm of imagination, intuition, clairvoyance, and other forms of "channeling" information. This phenomenon is sometimes called "seeing with your third eye," which implies a sort of psychic vision beyond our traditional understanding. This third eye, many believe, is not merely metaphorical. It is literally part of the brain, called the pineal gland, located in the middle of the skull (between the eyes).

The exact purpose of this small, pine cone–shaped gland is debated. Many researchers believe it is our window to wisdom, intuition, and extrasensory perception. Perhaps this is the reason why, throughout history, the pine cone has been used as a symbol of human enlightenment. In ancient Egypt, the Staff of Osiris, also known as the Staff of Hermes, depicted two intertwining snakes rising to meet at a pine cone. This symbol lives on today, both in our symbol for DNA and the medical symbol of the staff and serpents. The early art of Christianity, Hinduism, and Buddhism also depict numerous unexplained images of pine cones. This tradition lives on in modern religious symbolism. It is customary for the Roman Pope to carry a staff with a pine cone on the top. Is it possible that this pine cone represents the pineal gland, our third eye and connection to our inner vision?

Some modern scholars have made a connection between the lost knowledge of the pineal gland and our new understanding of psychedelic substances. It has been theorized by researcher Rick Strassman, MD, that the pineal gland produces the chemical compound DMT, also known as the "spirit molecule." Even in tiny amounts, DMT generates profound visions and dreamlike experiences. This theory suggests that, while we sleep, the pineal gland secretes trace amounts of DMT into the brain, causing us to enter the dream state.

Whether or not the imagination is projected by the pineal gland, the ability to imagine is a portal that connects our consciousness to worlds that cannot be seen. And just as we can strengthen and condition the body, we can also strengthen and condition the third eye.

How to download creative ideas.

My best ideas seldom come from my conscious mind; they jump into my head subconsciously. My main job as an artist is to widen my perception to cast a bigger net into the sea of ideas. Whether I am working on a book, a poem, a presentation, a client project, or a meme, I use the following process to activate my imagination.

1. Calm your nervous system

Imagination starts in the body. Our energy and nerves have a direct impact on our thoughts. Take time to create a calm and relaxing environment. Focus on your breath. Tell yourself that you are safe. You could even prepare by dancing, exercising, or vigorously shaking your body. When the body feels good, the mind follows.

2. Clear your mental clutter

Too much information leaves no space for inspiration. Imagination is found in the clear sky above the clouds of the cluttered mind. That's why meditation and mindfulness are huge benefits to the creative process. Still waters run deep. So does a still mind.

3. Give your ego a different job

The ego is the overanalytical voice inside your head. The ego isn't bad. It's only trying to help. But judgment and criticism can hinder imagination. Instead of suppressing the ego's need for control, make a deal with it. Tell the ego that it will have a chance to inspect and edit once you are finished. The details come last, and the ego is great with details.

4. Ask the universe a question

It has been said that prayer is talking to God, whereas meditation is listening to God. Asking the universe a question is similar to prayer. We simply direct our awareness to a particular topic and wait for a response. For example, you can ask the universe what message it might have for you, or what message the world needs from you.

5. Suspend your disbelief

Imagination includes a certain element of fantasy. Let yourself play without rules or restrictions. It's sort of like watching a movie. You have to suspend your disbelief in order to enjoy watching the story unfold. When it comes to imagination, it's okay to believe the impossible.

6. Listen to the space between your thoughts

Imagination is not about imposing your own ideas. It's about allowing ideas to come to you. Instead of listening to your thoughts, try tuning your awareness into the empty space *between* your thoughts. Let your mind float up into the sky, far away. When your intuition speaks, it will be soft, like a whisper. Try to sense with your full body instead of only thinking with your brain.

7. Trust what comes through

Write down ideas exactly as they come without censorship or editing. You might feel the urge to doubt or second-guess whatever pops into your head, but the more you get out of your own way, the more directly your imagination can communicate. Over time, I've learned to write down exactly what comes to me, whether my conscious mind likes it or not. I often look back on snippets of writing and wonder where they came from.

8. Hold the vision in your mind

In the early stages of conception, ideas are fickle. You can blink and they're gone. It's important to nurture your imagination by holding on to your ideas tightly. If you have a vision of something you want to create, hold the vision in your mind until it comes into higher and higher clarity.

9. Let go of expectations

Creativity requires a delicate balance of holding on and letting go. At a certain point, once the vision has been firmly planted in the subconscious, it's important to drop attachments to any specific outcome. Letting go of expectations frees you to act and create in the moment, which is where magic happens.

10. Dwell in gratitude

Living in gratitude will help you attract things into your life, including creative ideas. Imagine that your creative project is already finished. It's been launched into the world. How do you feel? Are you relieved? Excited? Thankful? Find that feeling now, and carry it with you throughout the creative process.

Turning imagination into results.

Of course, imagination alone isn't enough. We have to take actionable steps to bring our ideas to life. While I was sitting on the white sand of Flamenco Beach, publishing a book didn't seem realistic. After all, I was broke, unemployed, and stranded on a remote island. But I held the vision in my mind until it seemed possible, then started working toward the goal.

After a month on the island, I ended up back in New York City after a friend invited me to sleep on his couch. I started writing every day. On days when I felt happy, I wrote. On days when I felt discouraged, I wrote. Even though my chances of getting published were next to zero,

I continued to hold the vision in my mind. I even designed a book cover and printed it out. I looked at the cover every day, implanting the image in my subconscious.

When you choose to follow your imagination, you can't always see the road ahead. You might have a vision of a final destination, but the pathway remains unknown. As you trust yourself and hold the vision, the direction will be revealed step by step as you stumble forward in the dark.

The normal process of getting a book published goes as follows:

1. Build an audience around your expertise.

2. Develop a book proposal.

3. Find a literary agent.

4. Pitch your proposal to publishers.

5. Write the book.

I was going about it entirely backwards. I didn't have an audience or an expertise, let alone a literary agent. Yet I continued to write every day while simultaneously trying to grow my audience. There was a book inside me that wanted to come out. So, I made a deal with the universe. *It's my job to write the book*, I said, *and it's your job to get the book out into the world. I'll keep doing my job and let you do your job.*

A year later, my life in New York City had stabilized. I was working as a brand strategist for an advertising agency on Madison Avenue and living on the Upper East Side. Although I was busy with my day job, I continued working on my book each morning and night, accompanied by either a hot cup of coffee or a cool glass of wine. And little by little, my audience started to grow as I shared snippets of my work-in-progress book on social media.

Finally, I decided to put together a book proposal. When I finished, I sent the proposal to every agent and publisher I could find. The silence I received in response was deafening. Most people didn't even take time to reject my proposal. They didn't respond at all. I was discouraged, but I kept the vision in my imagination and continued writing, one cup of coffee, one glass of wine at a time.

While my book proposal was out with agents, I also sent it to a few friends for feedback, including Jake, the friend who had invited me to Culebra. Jake had recently crossed paths with an editor from the London office of a well-known publishing house. Without telling me, Jake gave her my book proposal. She must have liked it, because she passed it along to the publisher's New York headquarters.

I was riding a southbound 6 Train when I received the email. The publisher's editorial director had received my book proposal and wanted to know if I was available to meet the following day. My first reaction was confusion, followed by shock and, finally, gratitude. Tension dissolved from my body like an avalanche falling from a mountain.

How did she find me? I wondered. *I don't even have an agent.*

I tried to play it cool. Doing my best to blend in with the crowded subway, I assumed the official New York City commuter stance: head down, poker face, indifferent frown. But my act was a failure. I couldn't stop smiling.

> "Yes, I am a dreamer. For a dreamer is one who can only find his way by moonlight, and his punishment is that he sees the dawn before the rest of the world."

OSCAR WILDE

Sovereign consciousness.

As it turns out, what I thought was the worst thing that ever happened to me (becoming homeless and stranded on Culebra) was the best thing that ever happened to me (launching my career as an author). *Sh#t Your Ego Says* was published in 2017 and became a cult favorite. Being a published author opened new doors for me, such as public speaking, podcast interviews, and paid endorsement opportunities. A short time earlier, none of this seemed possible, but I held the vision in my imagination until it became real.

Imagination is a natural and vital part of being human. It enables us to see beyond the scope of the five senses and summon the visions we wish to manifest. Being a dreamer isn't a waste of time. Dreamers are brave explorers of consciousness, the bringers of new light.

The imagination is always working, whether we realize it or not. Like breath or emotions, it is automatic. But when we suppress our imagination, it will express itself in unexpected ways, similar to suppressed emotions. When we suppress pain or trauma, they can reveal themselves as hate or anger. Similarly, worry is a form of suppressed imagination. So are fear and paranoia. It's important to steer our imagination with purpose and intention.

We live in a society that attempts to restrict our ability to dream outside the box. Value is measured by how well we can follow the rules and be productive. Substances that keep our consciousness narrow and focused, such as caffeine and alcohol, are normalized, while substances that expand our consciousness, such as cannabis and psychedelics, are restricted. This hyperrational mentality discourages us from exploring the depth of our consciousness, causing an epidemic of worry and anxiety—the shadow side of suppressed imagination.

The role of the artist is to help restore the sovereign consciousness of humanity. Our job is to use the power of imagination to see beyond the arbitrary confines of social conventions to plant the seeds of a better future. Your dreams are medicine for the world.

Project visualization

Before starting a project (or whenever you feel stuck), sit in a comfortable position, close your eyes, and imagine the completed result. What would be the best possible outcome? Don't hold back. No vision is too big. Imagine every detail. What does the finished project look like? How do you feel? Who is celebrating with you? What is the public feedback? Dwell on the best possible scenario. Be as specific as possible. Hold the vision in your mind for five to ten minutes.

Now take a piece of paper and write a thank-you letter to the universe, expressing gratitude. "Dear universe, thank you for . . ."

Life hack:

Train your mind

to dwell on

beautiful

 thoughts

WORRY IS

A MISUSE OF

IMAGINATION

MY MIND AFTER
MEDITATION

MY MIND BEFORE
MEDITATION

Chapter 7

INTERVENTION WITH MY INNER CRITIC

I CAN BE my own worst critic. I tend to hold myself to high, sometimes unrealistic, standards and get down on myself for not living up to my own expectations. We all have an inner critic that attempts to pick apart our work—and often our self-esteem along with it. This nagging voice has stopped many creatives dead in their tracks.

A little self-doubt is good for you. It builds character and keeps you motivated to improve. For example, basketball legend Michael Jordan paid close attention to criticism from the media and other players. As great as he already was, he was always looking for a naysayer to prove wrong. This mentality helped him get better and better, adding new elements to his game year after year. If a creative person believes they have everything figured out, they might stop exploring. And art without exploration says nothing new, nothing exciting. It helps to have a little resistance, a little friction, to push back against.

However, too much self-doubt is never good. We have to acknowledge the inner critic, say *Thank you for your input*, and proceed anyway. The mind is like the weather, always changing, and we must have the determination to persevere through all conditions, the rain and sunshine alike.

As we wrap up talking about the yin stages of creative being and move into the yang stages of creative *doing*, it's time to move from stillness to action, from the inner world to the outer world. It's time to get to work. The following is a dialogue between the inner critic and the inner child to help you move past the resistance of getting started.

The inner critic versus the inner child.

Inner critic: I'm not talented enough.

Inner child: Your creativity is a unique expression of who you are: your experience and perspective. It doesn't make sense to compare yourself to anyone else. Nobody can offer exactly what you can. Besides, talent needs to be developed. The more you play around and experiment, the better you'll get. Don't worry about perfection. There is no such thing. Just try to develop your own unique style and voice.

Inner critic: Okay, but what's the point? I'm not a professional artist. Creativity feels like a waste of time.

Inner child: Creativity can improve several aspects of your life. Developing your creative, problem-solving capacity will benefit your career, your relationships, and your overall well-being. Besides, your soul wants to create. It's part of your nature. Give your art as an offering to the world.

Inner critic: But what if people hate what I make?

Inner child: I promise that nobody will judge you more harshly than you judge yourself. The truth is that most people are far too preoccupied with obsessing over themselves to pay much attention to what other people are doing. Fear of criticism is often a projection of our own self-doubt. Besides, feedback is helpful to your creative development. While you shouldn't obsess over other people's feedback and criticism, learning how your work is received and perceived will make you a better artist.

Inner critic: Makes sense. But I'm overwhelmed with possibilities and don't know where to start.

Inner child: Don't worry about making the wrong decision. Just make a decision. There is no right or wrong place to start. Overthinking kills the magic. Trust your instinct. Too much analysis leads to paralysis. Just start and see what happens. Move with faith, not fear. Let curiosity guide you. Seek to discover, not to achieve. One idea will lead to another. There is no right or wrong way. There is only one step at a time and the path you pave for yourself. Let it unfold without force or judgment. Make it fun. Keep it light. Creativity is no big deal.

Inner critic: Okay, I started. But now I keep getting stuck in the details.

Inner child: You're too early in the process to worry about the details. The details come last. Tell your ego to take a break. Give it reassurance that it will have a chance to review and perfect the work later. Now is the time to get your ideas out without overanalyzing them. Bad work is easier to fix than no work. Start with the big picture and get more detailed as you go.

Inner critic: Okay, maybe I have nothing to worry about. I'll just keep going and see what happens.

Inner child: Now you're getting it.

FEAR

KILLS

MORE

DREAMS

THAN

FAILURE

DOUBT SAYS	CREATIVITY SAYS
I'M AFRAID TO FAIL	I CAN'T FAIL, I'M JUST PLAYING
SEEMS LIKE A LOT OF WORK	HOW CAN I MAKE IT FUN?
I DON'T FEEL INSPIRED	I'LL START AND SEE WHAT HAPPENS
MY STYLE IS NOT PERFECT	MY QUIRKS MAKE ME UNIQUE
WHAT IF PEOPLE DON'T LIKE IT?	FEEDBACK MAKES ME BETTER
TRAUMA IS HOLDING ME BACK	EXPRESSION IS HEALING

PART TWO

YANG: CREATIVE DOING

Chapter 8

THE MYTH OF PERFECTION

"Do not fear mistakes. There are none."

MILES DAVIS

TO SAY I was nervous would be an understatement. I felt like a cat being thrown into cold water. My first book had been published days earlier, and this was my first television interview. At least I was prepared. My talking points were memorized, my notes were arranged in front of me, and I had finished three cups of strong coffee. I was wearing my cleanest white shirt. For a fifteen-minute interview, this may have been excessive. But I didn't care. I wanted it to be perfect.

At least I was comfortably at home. The interview was happening via live video conference. I was sitting in my Upper East Side apartment, my body tense from too much caffeine. I took one last look at my notes and sat down in front of my computer, waiting for the interview to start.

"We're going live in three . . . two . . . one . . ."

It was a train wreck. I had wanted to sound like an expert, but it came across as too rehearsed, too forced. I looked down to check my notes multiple times. Instead of speaking from the heart, I was aiming for an artificial idea of perfection that only existed inside my mind. It just wasn't natural.

I had wanted to look like a rising literary star, and I did. But contrary to my hopes, I was closer to the Latin word for "bad star"—*disaster*—combusting into a reckless supernova of gas and ego. I had to take a shower after the interview to wash off the stench, after which I crashed onto my bed and fell asleep, the sharp comedown from too much coffee.

Real is better than perfect.

One of the biggest roadblocks for creatives is the daunting pursuit of perfection. We often put unnecessary pressure on ourselves to live up to ideals that only exist inside our heads. This pressure manifests as all sorts of negative inner dialogue: *I'm not good enough. Someone else does it better. I don't have the proper training. I'm too critical of my own work. I'm afraid of getting bad feedback. What if they laugh at me?*

As creatives, we can be our own biggest critics. The desire for approval and perfection can be daunting. But how do we measure perfection? Who decides what is perfect? We sometimes call great art "perfect" in hindsight, but the process of making art (just like the process of life) is never perfect. Art is an act of spontaneity, not overanalysis. Art is messy. Art is experimentation. Art is curiosity looking for trouble and fun. During the moment of creation, it's best not to worry about the end result. You're not looking for a final solution. You're going on a journey. You're looking to discover something inside yourself. Never aim for external standards of perfection. The pursuit of perfection will only weigh you down. Instead, aim for discovery. Aim for play. Aim for freedom from the inner critic who says you must be perfect.

Art and creativity are a matter of subjective taste. Some people hear perfection in the raw guitar chords of punk-rock music. Some prefer the sloppy brushstrokes of abstract expressionism over polished realism. Poetry that speaks in emotive fragments can be more impactful than highly technical, grammatically correct stanzas. Often the most successful business people are those who let down their guard and reveal their human side, despite pressure to conform to a stubborn idea of professionalism. What one person perceives as messy, another person will find inspirational. Being real is better than being perfect.

In 1965, The Rolling Stones recorded a demo of a new song called "(I Can't Get No) Satisfaction." At the time, they didn't give the song much thought. It was just a demo. They intended to go back to the studio later to finish the recording, but their manager had other plans. He took the demo tape and released it to radio stations without the band's knowledge. Within days, the song was being played on radio stations across the United Kingdom. The Rolling Stones never returned to the studio to finish the song. The demo tape became the final version, and "(I Can't Get No) Satisfaction" would become one of the most iconic songs in rock 'n' roll history.

How would "(I Can't Get No) Satisfaction" sound if The Rolling Stones had gone back to the studio to re-record the demo? We'll never know. It's quite possible that the song would have lost some of the rough and raw energy that makes it so popular.

Art and creativity are transmissions of energy. Energy speaks louder than words. We react to art with our subconscious mind before we analyze it with our conscious mind. It's about expressing yourself and your message as directly as possible, in the language that comes most naturally to you. Your authentic nature is an energetic vibration. Your creativity is the vessel that transmits this vibration. One passionate sentence spoken from the heart speaks louder than a hundred pages of dry and polished script. Your authenticity is your most valuable currency.

The subtle art of perfect imperfection.

Perfection is an elusive concept. When we try too hard to make something perfect, we accidentally suck the life out of it. Imagine a spotless house with no trace of human touch. On the surface, it might look "perfect," but it isn't real. It's lacking warmth and feeling. True perfection, paradoxically, requires a degree of imperfection.

This paradox is captured by the Japanese concept of wabi-sabi, an approach to aesthetics that embraces quirks and imperfection. In the tradition of wabi-sabi, things like asymmetry, roughness, and cracks are part of an object's charm. This aesthetic was derived from Zen Buddhism, which teaches that all things are impermanent and in a constant state of decay and transition. Appreciating the beauty of imperfection is a way to recognize and embrace the impermanence of life.

The record producer Sam Phillips is often called the inventor of rock 'n' roll music. His Memphis recording studio, Sun Studio, gave birth to some of the biggest musical hits of the 1950s, launching the careers of people like B. B. King, Jerry Lee Lewis, Ike Turner, and Johnny Cash. Phillips was constantly searching for what he called "perfect imperfection," a lively balance of the structured and the unexpected.

In 1951, a Mississippi band called Kings of Rhythm traveled to Memphis to record some new songs. On their way, their amplifier fell out of their truck and broke on the pavement. Once they reached Sun Studio, Phillips began experimenting with the broken amp to achieve new sounds, eventually filling it with newspaper. The resulting sound was a muffled and distorted hum—the first ever use of reverb in recorded music. The track, "Rocket 88," is now considered the first rock 'n' roll song.

Sam Phillips's pursuit of perfect imperfection helped to define the most popular music genre of the twentieth century. He once selected a take for the sole reason that a telephone was ringing in the background, creating a natural and unexpected ambiance. Phillips considered this approach to be aligned with the natural world, which achieves an organic beauty without human interference. It was this philosophy that gave Phillips the instinct to make music with an unknown, rough-around-the-edges truck driver named Elvis Presley, whose unique blend of perfect imperfection and wild dancing hips would change music forever.

The wisdom of instinct.

The human mind is a delicate balance between spontaneity and control. In psychology, these are represented by the id and the ego. Each plays an important role. The id represents our natural instincts and impulses. The ego keeps these instincts and impulses in check so that we can manage our relationships and fit into an organized society. For example, if you feel hungry, your id might want to scream and cry like a baby until somebody feeds you. The ego is there to remind you that an important business meeting is not the right place to start screaming.

Although the ego and id are both important, the controlling force of ego has taken a dominant role in our society. On an institutional and individual level, control is prioritized over instinct and expression. This may be good for top-down control systems, but it's bad for human freedom and creativity. It's no wonder we are afraid of making mistakes. We are conditioned to listen to the judgmental ego over our natural intuition.

The process of reawakening the inner artist includes a systematic unlearning of the social constructs we have been taught, including the need for control. The practices of Buddhism, including meditation, are designed to quiet the ego and deepen our connection with instinct. American novelist Jack Kerouac was inspired by Buddhism when he developed a writing philosophy called "spontaneous prose."

When writing his celebrated novels, such as *On the Road*, Kerouac did his best to ignore the critical ego and let words flow through him without hesitation or judgment. "First thought, best thought" was his mantra. Kerouac's creative process involved sitting at his typewriter and letting his fingers hit the keys as quickly as possible, like a jazz saxophonist improvising in the moment. He didn't give himself a chance to overanalyze or doubt his prose. And though Kerouac's writing was not always polished or tidy, his stories jumped off the page with energy and emotion. He transmitted a clear and powerful vibration with each sentence. It was instinct set free: a rejection of the ego's desire to micromanage the process. The result was hugely popular, a breath of fresh air in the world of literature.

Early in his career, Allen Ginsberg (Kerouac's friend) wrote very formulaic and polished poetry. It was decent poetry in a traditional sense, but it had yet to find an audience. Everything changed in 1955 when Ginsberg decided to test Kerouac's mantra—*first thought, best thought.* He sat down in his Lower East Side apartment and started typing the poem that would become "Howl," beginning with the famous words, "I saw the best minds of my generation destroyed by madness."

For the first time, Ginsberg allowed the words to flow through him without interference from his inner critic. He described the process like his subconscious mind was vomiting onto the page. There was no traditional structure, just a free-flowing and visionary collage of ideas. Images of sex, terror, and salvation filled stanza after unstructured stanza.

For Ginsberg, it was catharsis, a form of therapy. While writing the poem, he never intended to publish it. The writing was too personal, too raw, too naked. He felt embarrassed and exposed by the words and feelings he had expressed. Luckily for the world of literature, Ginsberg changed his mind. During a poetry reading in San Francisco, he decided to perform "Howl." The poem became an instant sensation. His honesty struck a chord with an entire generation and catapulted him into literary fame. Today, "Howl" is regarded as among the greatest poems of the twentieth century.

How to trust (and sharpen) your instinct.

My best ideas are usually spontaneous. They pop into my awareness without effort or force. Instinct is a sense of inner knowing. It's not a thought, per se, but a sensation. It lives in the body as much as the brain. Imagine a football quarterback. The game moves fast. Players are running in multiple directions. The defense is trying to tackle him. The quarterback only has a matter of seconds to make a decision.

Will he throw the ball? Will he run? How much power does he put into the pass? How does he calculate how to find the right receiver and avoid the defense?

The landscape of the football field shifts rapidly. The quarterback must make numerous risk/opportunity assessments in a split second. How is this achieved? Through instinct. Instinct is the mind's superpower to evaluate hundreds of microdecisions simultaneously—nearly unconsciously—and derive the best course of action.

Instinct is both natural and a learned skill. We all have the capacity for instinct, but it grows stronger with experience and practice. For example, an experienced quarterback who has played hundreds of games has already faced nearly every scenario. The lessons of multiple mistakes and successes are stored in his subconscious. His instinct has more data to draw from. By contrast, a younger quarterback may have tremendous physical talent and intelligence, but without the wisdom of lived experience, his instinct might be underdeveloped, resulting in miscalculations. This is what we call a "rookie mistake."

Our instinct is forged by experience. The goal is not to always succeed. The goal is to master the game. And failure is an essential lesson on the road to mastery. Whatever you want to do, start *now*, before you're ready. Do something outlandish. Push against the edge of your comfort zone. Give your instinct more data points to work with.

Jazz and the art of improvisation.

When we listen to our instinct, we tap into wisdom beyond the conscious mind. This is similar to the intuitive nature of children before their egos are fully developed. They somehow possess insight that seems otherworldly, as if they are still connected to whatever mysterious realm they originated from prior to being born—just the way an idea itself lives in a state of ethereal limbo before being manifested on Earth through a creator.

WILLIAM S. BURROUGHS

All creativity, to a degree, is an act of channeling. The mind is a natural antenna for ideas and inspiration. The best ideas don't need to be forced. They come naturally when we are in a state of receptivity. Practicing the art of improvisation—acting in the moment without censorship or fear of mistakes—is one way to sharpen our ability to channel ideas.

An example of spontaneous creativity can be seen in the evolution of jazz music. At the turn of the twentieth century, ragtime was the most popular style of music in America. It was composed as written sheet music and regarded as the folk-American equivalent to European classical music. It was lively music for its time, but every line was meticulously planned in advance, note by note.

Ragtime took a huge leap forward when innovative musicians in places like New Orleans, Kansas City, and Chicago started experimenting with unplanned melodies mid-performance. The music suddenly jumped from the written page and came alive as spontaneous human expression. The result was sometimes sloppy, but always refreshing and honest. No mistake or emotion was hidden. This new style came to be known as jazz. By comparison, ragtime sounded stale.

We as creatives too often remain stuck on the written page, afraid of making a mistake. But sometimes what we perceive as a mistake is actually a portal to an exciting and unexpected destination we wouldn't have discovered otherwise.

Spontaneous mind.

A few weeks after my (embarrassing) television interview, I was shocked when they asked me to return for another segment. *They must be kidding*, I thought. *Are they trying to torture me? Are they trying to torture their audience?* Remembering how badly my first interview had gone, I almost declined. But I remembered something that a comedian friend once told me.

"Failure is guaranteed to happen," she said. "You have to fail before you can succeed. New comedians are terrible for two or three years. But failure is good training because it helps you get comfortable on stage. The best thing a young comedian can do is fail as many times as possible as early as possible. Once you're no longer afraid to fail, you're finally ready to succeed."

I wasn't a comedian, but I knew how it felt to be the punchline of a bad joke, so I decided to take her advice. The following days passed quickly. I tried to not worry about the upcoming interview. Soon I stopped thinking about it entirely, a decision that would come back to haunt me.

My alarm rang on Monday morning. I woke up alone in my Upper East Side apartment. Outside I could hear the bustling sounds of 72nd Street. I rolled over in bed and looked at my iPhone. "You have one event today," an alert said. "Your interview is scheduled to start in fifteen minutes."

Interview?

It took a few seconds to remember.

Today? Oh no.

I had tried so hard to forget about the interview that I had literally forgotten the date. It was today. It was starting in fifteen minutes. And I was still in bed.

Every cell in my body rallied together under a single emotion: panic. I jumped out of bed and ran to my closet to put on the cleanest shirt I could find. I buttoned my shirt with one hand while brushing my teeth with the other. I needed to shave but there wasn't time. There was only time for essentials, and not all of those.

I set my computer in a corner of my apartment with good lighting. My heart was racing. What was I forgetting? Coffee! I boiled water and dumped coffee into my French press. Hardly a day had gone by over the past decade when I hadn't started my morning with a strong cup of coffee. This was no day to make an exception. I sat down in front of my computer to test my camera, adjusting the frame while waiting for the water to boil. I had five minutes.

I had managed to (mostly) prepare myself physically, but mentally I was still adrift. What would I say? How would I say it? I searched for the notes that I had prepared for the first interview, but I couldn't find them. I checked the clock. The coffee wouldn't be ready in time. I wasn't wearing pants. It would be me alone with my naked, spontaneous mind.

I closed my eyes. *Inhale. Exhale. Inhale. Exhale.*

"We're going live in three . . . two . . . one . . ."

What choice did I have? I channeled my inner jazz musician. I improvised. There was no time to pretend to be anyone other than myself. I had no words prepared so I made them up on the spot. When I was younger, I used to have a recurring dream of being naked while giving a presentation in front of a large audience. This was just as uncomfortable, except it was inescapably real.

"We're here with James McCrae," the interviewer said, "an expert on ego and creativity . . ."

"Thanks for, uh, having me," I stuttered. "But I would never, uh, I would never call myself an expert. That is, I'm just a writer. I write from personal experience. But, yeah, I'm not exactly an expert on anything."

The host looked at me blankly before moving on, dumbfounded that I had derailed a simple introduction.

The next fifteen minutes were the longest fifteen minutes of my life. I don't remember many details. I said things that probably sounded stupid. But it was better than I expected, even better than my first interview. At least I had been myself, embarrassingly so. Instead of anxiously trying to remember the right words and coming across as rigid and insincere, I allowed the words to flow through me without hesitation or judgment.

During my first interview, I had been striving for perfection, but maybe that was the wrong approach. What if, like a jazz band, perfection was the wrong measure of success? What if there was no universal standard to measure myself against, only the zig-zagging line of personal progress and discovery? I may not be perfect, but that's okay. I'm just a human being trying to figure things out like everybody else. And that's enough.

Listening to the busy sounds of Manhattan outside my window, I tried not to think about how stupid I may have sounded during the interview. After all, I was starting to suspect that it was worry and overthinking that had caused my anxiety in the first place. Maybe if I could learn to simply remain still and listen, the words I needed would come naturally.

I returned to my French press to finally pour a cup of coffee. Later, I put on pants.

CREATIVE PLAYTIME

Spontaneous writing

Sit down in a comfortable position, close your eyes, and meditate for ten minutes. Simply focus on your breath, each inhale and exhale. If your mind wanders, let it wander, then slowly come back to focusing on the breath. Immediately after this meditation, pick up a pen and a notebook and start writing. Don't worry about what to write. Jot down the first thing that pops into your mind and keep going. It doesn't have to make logical sense. Let your subconscious mind be purged onto the paper. Write continuously for ten minutes without lifting up your pen. There are no wrong results.

Here are a few prompts to fuel your writing:

- What is the universe trying to tell me?

- What sort of energy am I feeling right now?

- What message does the world need at this moment?

After ten minutes, look at what you wrote and circle any key words or phrases that stand out: anything that feels relevant or emotionally charged. These are the messages that your subconscious is trying to express. Next, if you desire, construct a poem using the words and phrases you circled.

Bad idea dump

Whatever you're working on, try making it bad. Really bad. Write down as many bad ideas as possible. If you're a visual artist, make an intentionally bad drawing. If you're a comedian, write bad jokes. If you're looking for a book title, think of intentionally bad names. This will get the wheels turning and take the pressure off. And one of your bad ideas might turn out to be unexpectedly brilliant.

FORGET PERFECTION

THE PROCESS IS MORE IMPORTANT

THAN THE RESULTS

DROP EXPECTATIONS. MESS IT UP.

HAVE FUN. GET LOST.

MAKE THINGS WITH THE CARELESS

ABANDON OF A CHILD

JUMP IN BEFORE YOU'RE READY

START NOW

IT'S NOT ABOUT BEING GOOD AT CREATIVITY

IT'S ABOUT CREATIVITY BEING GOOD FOR YOU

A MIND TOO FULL OF INFORMATION HAS NO SPACE FOR INSPIRATION

(figure A)

(figure B)

CREATIVITY IS INTELLIGENCE HAVING FUN

Chapter 9

FINDING YOUR STYLE

"A genius is the one most like himself."

THELONIOUS MONK

CONTENT IS WHAT you say. Style is how you say it. When it comes to creativity, style is just as important as content. Your style is your unique fingerprint, the flavor only you can create. Many artists share a similar message or idea, but style sets them apart.

Style is a matter of personal preference and taste. In every type of art, there is room for numerous styles to peacefully coexist. Mastering your style is not about having the most talent. It's about developing a voice that is uniquely your own. Your style could be subtle, quiet, minimal, bold, sincere, funny, sarcastic, or provocative. There is no objectively good or bad style. It's about finding the voice that feels most natural.

As Charles Bukowski once said, "Style is the answer to everything. A fresh way to approach a dull or dangerous thing. To do a dull thing with style is preferable to doing a dangerous thing without it. To do a dangerous thing with style is what I call art."

There is no right or wrong style.

One of the most unique stylistic innovators in twentieth-century art is the painter Andy Warhol. One of the reasons his style is so unique is because it is no style at all in some ways; rather, it's an exact replication of pop-culture iconography. Coming from a background as a graphic designer for fashion publications, including *Vogue*, Warhol developed a knack for simple, whimsical commercial art. In the 1960s, he took his designs from the magazine to the museum, filling avant-garde galleries in downtown New York with paintings of Campbell's soup cans, Marilyn Monroe, cows, hamburgers, and Elvis Presley—none of which were considered appropriate subject matter for "serious" art.

To make his style even more distinct, Warhol replaced his paintbrush with silk-screen technology, eliminating the human element of brushstrokes, making his art seem cold and mechanical. It has been said that Warhol's art is devoid of personal expression but is rather an ironic and detached form of social commentary. He was reflecting back the aesthetics and priorities of the increasingly commercialized United States. Warhol's style, although controversial at the time, came to define the second half of the twenthieth century.

Stylistic movements go in and out of fashion. Sincerity is popular in one decade; irony and detachment are popular the next decade. Minimalism and restraint have a season. So do excess and flash. The pendulum is always swinging back and forth. The style of Andy Warhol and the pop art genre he pioneered could not have been more different than the art movement that preceded it, abstract expressionism—a style known for wild, emotive brushstrokes.

Jackson Pollock was the figurehead of abstract expressionism. His style was just as distinct as Warhol's, but on the opposite end of the stylistic spectrum. Whereas Warhol was anti-expressive, Pollock was hyper-expressive. He flung paint at canvases with wild abandon, usually with a cigarette hanging from his lips. It was a physical, masculine, even violent style of painting that reflected the hero archetype of the 1950s: the stoic man's man, commander of his own destiny, as popularized in John Wayne movies and Ayn Rand novels. (This archetype would be challenged in the 1960s by the sexual revolution, feminism, and queer icons like Andy Warhol. Cultural styles change as much as artistic styles. In fact, the two are often interconnected.)

Warhol and Pollock were extremely different, both as artists and as people, yet both achieved a masterful expression of personal aesthetic that cannot be duplicated by even the best imitators.

Style is cyclical. A popular style wears out its welcome, fades out of fashion, and returns again (perhaps decades later) in a new form. In the late 1970s, the youth in the United States and England had grown tired of the "flower power" music that had dominated the radio since The Beatles had helped to usher in the hippie movement over a decade earlier. A style and message that seems profound to one generation can feel trite and stale to the next.

It was a time of social and political degradation. The future looked bleak. The hippie dream had failed to enact meaningful systemic change. Looking for an artistic style that reflected the state of the world, a handful of visionary bands, such as The Ramones and The Clash, reached back to the early days of 1950s rock 'n' roll, stripping away all the ornate instrumentation, guitar solos, and flashy production, restoring rock music to its naked essence: three chords and a beat. This new style of music, which was an interpretation of an older style of music, came to be known as punk rock.

Some art is intentionally obscure, difficult, or unintelligible: for example, the absurdism of the Dada movement, the repetitive fragments of Gertrude Stein's poetry, the conceptual comedy of Andy Kaufman, or the distorted chaos of noise rock. The purpose of such art is not to provide a pleasant audience experience, but rather to push stylistic boundaries and challenge convention. The meaning (if any does exist) is cloaked behind layers of stylistic abstraction, and the style itself is often the point.

The Irish novelist James Joyce is considered one of the greatest stylistic innovators in literary history. In his 1920 masterpiece *Ulysses*, Joyce dedicated more than 250,000 words to a single day in the life of the protagonist, providing a detailed exploration of the inner world of consciousness, which was so shocking at the time that it was banned upon publication.

But it was in another novel, *Finnegans Wake*, that Joyce pushed his stylistic boundaries to the extreme. While *Finnegans Wake* is considered brilliant by literary critics, it is most famous for being utterly unreadable. The language itself changes inexplicably mid-chapter without warning or explanation. The rules of spelling and grammar are thrown out the window. The perspective and timeline jump around erratically. There is no plot to speak of, and even a deep analysis inspires more questions than answers. But despite the novel's difficulty, it is studied and admired as a great work of literature.

To get a small taste of the style of *Finnegans Wake*, here are the opening sentences:

> riverrun, past Eve and Adam's, from swerve of shore to bend of bay, brings us by a commodius vicus of recirculation back to Howth Castle and Environs. Sir Tristram, violer d'amores, fr'over the short sea, had passencore rearrived from North Armorica on this side the scraggy isthmus of Europe Minor to wielderfight his penisolate war: nor had topsawyer's rocks by the stream Oconee exaggerated themselse to Laurens County's gorgios while they went doublin their mumper all the time: nor avoice from afire bellowsed mishe mishe totauftauf thuartpeatrick: not yet, though venissoon after, had a kidscad buttended a bland old isaac: not yet, though all's fair in vanessy, were sosie sesthers wroth with twone nathandjoe.

While this language may appear random to the casual observer, Joyce is following an internal logic of his own creation, like a code that must be cracked by the reader. There are no rules or limits as to what style is acceptable in art. No style is inherently right or wrong. Style is about individual flair and expression, an outward manifestation of the energy and emotions that reside within.

Give yourself permission to change.

Style is not a static thing. It can change and develop over time. Finding your style is like teenagers finding their fashion sense: it's awkward in the beginning. You might go through several phases before finding an aesthetic that works for you. The key is experimentation. You have to take risks and try new things in order to expand your comfort zone.

It's a good idea to master the fundamentals before getting too fancy. A child must walk before they can ride a bike. Before Pablo Picasso went on to revolutionize the art world with his warped abstraction, he was a classically trained realist painter. As a precocious teenager, he mastered the traditional style of landscapes and religious scenes before experimenting with form and perspective. Picasso continued to evolve his style over time, going through several distinct phases— the Blue Period, the Rose Period, primitivism, cubism, abstraction, and surrealism. He was in a perpetual state of self-invention, a state of becoming.

> "I knew who I was this morning, but I've changed a few times since then."
>
> LEWIS CARROLL

Your own voice is forever a work in progress. It will change as you change. We are all shaped and changed by our life experiences, and these experiences inform our art. Give yourself permission to change, both as a human and a creator. Reinvent yourself whenever you feel stuck or stale. It doesn't matter how old you are. Creativity has no age limit. It's never too late to evolve or try something new. Some artists, like Mozart, are fully formed by age eighteen. Others find their stride later in life. The country singer Johnny Cash had a long and legendary career as a young man before falling out of the spotlight, but with the help of producer Rick Rubin, Cash pulled off an exceptional comeback at age seventy. This music introduced an entirely new style to Cash's catalog, a style that was wise and weathered like a fine wine. It was among the most popular music of his career.

To be human—and especially to be an artist—is not a fixed experience. It is fluid and always changing. Every single cell in your body is in a constant state of death and regeneration. The seasons change. The moon moves in cycles. So do we. Don't limit yourself to being the person you have always been.

Inventing yourself.

In the modern world of social media, YouTube, and podcasting, having a unique style is as important as ever. When people are overstimulated with media and content, an original style and persona is how we stand out. It's important to embody your style and to project an intentional image and voice into the world.

It has been said that Andy Warhol's greatest work of art was himself. His persona was a character he carefully cultivated. No detail went unnoticed: his glasses, his wig, his outfits, his art studio, his speech and mannerisms. His personal style was an extension of his artistic style. They told the same story. Warhol's canvas was the entire world, including himself, and his artistic signature was imprinted in every single action and public appearance.

For some, crafting an image or persona can feel inauthentic, especially in the beginning, but the truth is that we are projecting an image or persona whether we realize it or not. Becoming a living embodiment of your art is about having self-awareness and purposefully showing up in the way you want to be perceived. This isn't an act. Your style will be more believable and create deeper connections when it is rooted in authenticity.

Think of yourself as your greatest work of art—one that is always changing and evolving. Step out from the shadows. Let yourself be seen and heard. You don't have to be cool, popular, or beautiful. Just as there are endless styles of captivating art, there are endless styles of captivating people. Turn up the volume on whatever comes naturally. Own your niche.

5 ways to craft a unique style.

1. Borrow from your heroes

Take a deeper look at your favorite creators. What are the defining attributes of their style? It could be the way they make things, the way they present themselves, or even the way they do business. Feel free to try out the techniques that resonate. That doesn't mean you should imitate or copy them. It means integrating their style into your work—bending and molding it like clay—until it becomes your own.

2. Master the fundamentals

Before basketball players can complete a flashy 360-degree dunk, they must learn to dribble and control the ball. Even if you want to create daring, experimental work, it helps to master the basics first. Once your home has a steady foundation, you can start decorating the walls.

3. Know yourself

What you create is an extension of your being. Ask yourself: *Who am I in the world? What is my purpose? What message do I have to share?*

How do I want to make people feel? Lean into your natural disposition—both your strengths and your weaknesses—to communicate with purpose and intention.

4. Expand your horizons

A person who has traveled the world will probably have a richer perspective and life experience than someone who has never left their hometown. Novelty expands us. It helps us see the world with fresh eyes. The more styles or aesthetics you practice, the more you can pull from as you develop a voice that represents your totality.

5. Continue to evolve

Don't get stuck in one place. As a person, you are always changing and growing. Let your art adapt to where you are today. Sometimes it takes a long time to develop a style and voice that are uniquely your own. Stay open. Stay curious. Give yourself permission to become somebody new.

Your authenticity is your currency.

Your very being is a vibration, a meme, a manifesto. What is the message you are projecting into the world with your art and your presence? Is there alignment between *what* you are saying and *how* you are saying it—your content and your style?

Everything we do and say projects a stylistic image. This is especially true of artists. Are you projecting your image by default? Are you copying someone else? Or are you cultivating your own style and voice with purpose and intention?

Don't worry about pleasing everyone. You can't be all things to all people. It's better to find a niche that is authentic to you, then continue to experiment and evolve as you grow as a person and a creator. If you are Jackson Pollock, don't worry about being Andy Warhol. If you are Andy Warhol, don't worry about being Jackson Pollock.

You can be yourself better than you can be anyone else.

Design a uniform

Pretend you have to choose a single outfit to wear for the rest of your life. What uniform would best exemplify your personal style? What shirt? What pants? What shoes, hat, or jewelry? Go through your closet and distill your wardrobe to its essence. Decide which outfit is the most you.

Now ask yourself: *How does this apply to my creativity? What does my personal style say about my creative style? How can I distill my creative output to my most unique essence?*

Make a moodboard

When I was working in branding, one of the first phases of each project was to make a moodboard, which is a way to identify and clarify your desired style prior to designing a new brand identity. The moodboard can be used by artists of all kinds to define a unifying tone or feeling for their work.

Moodboards can be made either digitally or physically. The first step is finding source material. You can search for images online (hint: Pinterest is a good resource) or cut them out of newspapers and magazines. The objective is to find images, colors, and words that evoke a mood or style that represents you. Create a visual collage with the images you find. Use this moodboard as a North Star as you develop and refine your style.

Create a character

It's time to channel your inner illustrator. Get a notebook or sketchbook and develop your own character. It can be a human, an animal, an alien, or any other fictional character. It can represent you or just be a figment of your imagination. Don't worry about technical skill. It can be a stick figure, a silly cartoon, or something more realistic. The point is to imbue your character with a style and personality that comes naturally to you.

Don't stop with your first sketch. Keep drawing and evolving your character until it feels complete. You can even give your character a name, a bio, a catchphrase, or dialogue. Now review your work and consider what this character says about your personal style.

"THE CREATIVE JOURNEY"

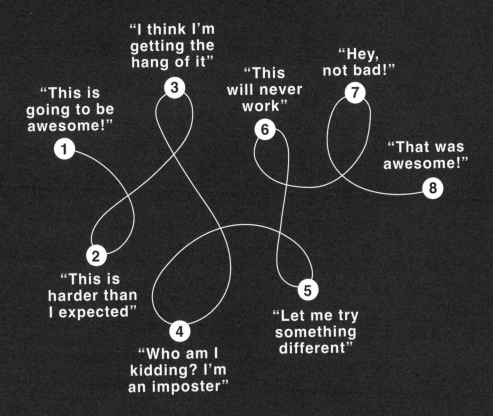

WHEN EVERYONE IS TRYING TO FIT IN

HAVE THE COURAGE TO STAND OUT

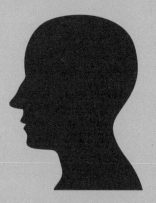

Chapter 10

INSPIRATION IS A HABIT

"Don't think about making art. Just get it done. Let everyone
else decide if it's good or bad, whether they love it or
hate it. While they are deciding, make even more art."

ANDY WARHOL

THE CREATIVE PROCESS is similar to farming. There's a time to prepare the soil, a time to plant the seeds, a time to harvest the crops, and a
time to eat the food. Intuition and imagination require action to bring the
process to fruition. The best idea in the world means nothing unless it can
be crafted into tangible form. Ideas are easy. Execution is what matters.

Bringing ideas to life doesn't necessarily require great talent. But
it does require practice and effort. And most importantly, it requires
showing up on a consistent basis, making your creative practice a habit.

When I work with clients to help them develop and launch creative
projects, one of the most common challenges I hear is the lack of inspiration. They are waiting for the right idea to come out of nowhere and
strike like a bolt of lightning. Until then, they are frozen, stuck in uncertainty, unsure where to begin.

I tell them to look for movement, not perfection. Any action is good
action. What we want to do is shake up the energy, create momentum,

and see what happens. Consistency is key. It doesn't matter if you write a thousand words or ten words. The point is to show up and put one foot in front of the other. We learn by doing. With action comes clarity. Lightning may indeed strike, but you need to be outside in the storm, not sitting on your couch watching TV.

As the painter Chuck Close said, "Inspiration is for amateurs. The rest of us just show up and get to work. If you wait around for the clouds to part and a bolt of lightning to strike you in the brain, you are not going to make an awful lot of work. All the best ideas come out of the process; they come out of the work itself."

My favorite sport is basketball. To me, it's the most creative sport. Like jazz music, basketball is a spontaneous synchronization between players. Anything could happen on any given play. The magic is created in the moment. One principle of a good basketball team is constant movement. An open shot doesn't just happen. It is created. Smart teams are always passing the ball, setting screens for teammates, and rotating around the court. It's impossible to see the entire play unfold in advance. Each small movement may seem inconsequential, but one pass leads to another. One rotation changes the dynamic of the court. And sooner or later, a hole in the defense is revealed. An open shot appears.

This approach is highly relevant to the creative process. Movement and momentum are essential. You don't have to have everything figured out before you start. One sentence leads to another, which leads to another. Purge your mind and see what happens. You can always make changes later. As one writer friend once told me, "It's easier to fix bad pages than no pages."

Building creative endurance.

Creativity is a muscle. The more you use it, the stronger it becomes. Most people who claim to be uncreative are simply out of shape. They haven't been exercising their creative muscles. But with training and dedication, anyone can become stronger, both physically and creatively.

When I was working in advertising, I developed a strong creative training routine. Every week there was another client deadline. Sitting around and waiting for inspiration wasn't an option. Overthinking was a luxury I couldn't afford. I needed to complete my projects on time. My clients had paid us good money and were eager to see the fruits of their investment.

While this demanding pace eventually took a toll on my mental health, it was good training to strengthen my creative muscles. I learned that deadlines can be helpful. When under pressure, the mind is capable of extraordinary ingenuity. The right idea can be plucked out of thin air. I also learned that overthinking does not always produce better results. The first idea is often the best idea. It's better to take an idea—any idea—and work with it, playing around to see where it leads you than it is to wallow in doubt and indecision. Execute and move on. Done is better than perfect.

These days, I give myself more room to breathe. I'm no longer driven by tight client deadlines. Nonetheless, I still show up every single morning to create. My morning routine consists of sitting down with an open notebook and waiting to see what happens. Some days are more productive than others. Several memes might come through, or a complete poem, or a full book chapter. Other days the muse remains quiet. I might write only a single paragraph—or perhaps nothing at all. To me, it doesn't make a difference. I don't give myself a strict word count to achieve. Consistency is more important than output. My job is to show up. What happens next is outside my control.

A baseball player who gets on base just one-third of the time is considered very successful. The same is true with creativity. Not everything you make will be your best work. You might go several days without making anything at all. That's okay. Keep showing up. The more times you swing the bat, the more chances you'll have to hit a home run.

Repetition creates habits. The more you dedicate yourself to something, the easier it becomes over time. Different times of day—and even different seasons of the year and phases of the moon—will affect your creativity in different ways. Our mood and mentality in July are different from our mood and mentality in January. As you develop your creative practice, notice how the energy in the world is affecting you. Work with whatever energy you are feeling. The singer-songwriter Neil Young likes to write during the full moon. He says that full-moon energy is rich and potent for the creative process, which helps him write better songs.

Achieving flow state.

Nobody starts out as an expert. The apprentice becomes the master through practice and persistence. In his book *Outliers: The Story of Success*, Malcolm Gladwell says that you need to spend ten thousand hours doing something in order to master it. It's about building muscle memory. The more times you do something, the easier it gets. Like riding a bike, your body remembers what to do.

Flow state is the condition of unconscious mastery. Your work flows automatically without conscious control. You know exactly what to do and how to do it because you've done it thousands of times before.

Think of an amazing dancer. During the dance, there is no time to think about each move in advance. It happens automatically—in flow. The mind was essential to learn the moves originally, but through practice and repetition, each step becomes ingrained in the body's memory. One move flows to the next without analysis.

Whatever your medium, think of your creativity like dancing. Learn the moves. Memorize them. Then practice, practice, practice so you can forget them.

How to get unstuck.

The creative process is seldom smooth sailing from beginning to end. There will be detours, wrong turns, distractions, and self-doubt. At times you might feel frozen in place, unsure how to proceed. Don't worry. Getting stuck is not an indication of failure. It's a normal part of the process for professionals and amateurs alike. Like all seasons, this too shall pass. The most important thing is to have patience with yourself. The creative process is not always linear. It's a winding road—and often a roller coaster. The best you can do is remain flexible and persistent as roadblocks arise. The following are some strategies to use whenever you feel stuck.

1. Use a different part of your brain

When we do something often, it creates a groove in the mind, similar to paving a dirt path into a nice smooth road. Taking a different route requires intentional effort. If you're feeling stuck, try giving your brain a new experience. If you're a scientist, try drawing. If you're an architect, try writing. Learn a new language. Developing new skills will forge new pathways, allowing you to see old problems from a fresh perspective.

2. Do something random

Creativity requires nonlinear thinking. Doing something random or spontaneous can help you escape a mental rut. Visit a random city, take a new route to work, listen to a new genre of music, or try a new cuisine. Watch a documentary about an artist you don't know much about. Open a book to a random page and see what message is waiting for you. Sometimes randomness is not random. Getting out of your own way and stopping the momentum of linear thought can open the door to divine intervention.

3. Treat it like a game

When we take creativity too seriously, which puts too much pressure on the outcome, the joy and pleasure get sucked out of the process, replaced by a sense of burden. When a child engages in creativity or play, they rarely get "stuck" because they don't burden themselves with expectations. It's all a game. It helps to lower the stakes. And ironically, when we take ourselves and our creations lightly, we arrive at a better and more fulfilling destination. As Jack Kerouac once said, "Enlightenment comes when you don't care."

4. Move your body

Creativity is the process of moving energy. This energy starts in the unseen world of ideas, is felt by your emotions, moves to your conscious mind, and is eventually released through the body. Feeling stuck implies that, somewhere along the process, the energy is not moving. There is a blockage. When this happens, it's helpful to move *any* energy. Shake your arms vigorously. Dance around your room. Go for a run. Take a yoga class. Or try something more subtle, like breath work. Do anything to disrupt your routine and get your energy moving.

5. Get a second opinion

Making art can be a lonely endeavor. When I'm deep into a creative project, I tend to isolate myself, lost in a world of my own creation. The problem with working alone is that you can only see challenges from a single point of view. It helps to receive feedback from a trusted friend or collaborator. One advantage of working for an advertising agency was having an entire team around me. The designers helped review the strategy. The copywriters helped review the design. Whether you work alone or as part of a team, it helps to be surrounded by a creative support system. This could be simply sharing your ideas with a trusted friend or family member.

6. Spend time in nature

The natural world provides a reset to the mind and the nervous system. Going for a hike in the woods or a swim in the ocean will calm your body and open your mind. One of my favorite ways to appreciate nature is to simply to bask in sunlight, preferably with as few clothes as possible. We absorb an unspoken intelligence whenever we make contact with nature. For those who can't get to a beach or a hike easily, go to a local park and simply sit down on the grass. Better yet, take off your shoes and socks, and let your feet ground into the earth for a few minutes. Or simply step outside your apartment and go for a walk around your neighborhood, listening to the sounds around you.

7. Ask the universe for guidance

There is strength in surrender, but surrender is not about quitting. It's about giving up the need for egoic control and aligning your intentions with higher wisdom. There is no right or wrong way to ask the universe for guidance. You could pray, meditate, or write down a question in your notebook and quietly wait for an answer. The important thing is to get out of your own way and allow yourself to be guided. Surrender is the portal.

The hunting instinct.

Having a dedicated creative practice fulfills the ancient human need to hunt, to explore, and to discover. For most of history, humans were hunters and gatherers. Our minds were stimulated by the daily pursuit of essential goals. We roamed the prairie and jungle in a constant state of exploration.

Today, in our highly sterilized society, there is little activity to stimulate our primal hunting instincts. Our jobs and socializing often involve staring at computer screens for hours on end. Our food is packaged and delivered from far away. Our supply chains are automated. We are disconnected from nature, from the wild. And we attempt to simulate the thrill of the hunt by playing video games, watching sports, and fixating on gossip and interpersonal drama. But these artificial substitutes fail to scratch the itch. Our deeply embedded desire to hunt and explore with purpose is left unmet, leading to large-scale depression and anxiety.

It is my belief and my experience that a genuine commitment to creativity can stimulate our instincts for hunting and adventure better than almost anything else. The search for new ideas, new inspiration, and new creation never ends. Every morning I wake up excited by the prospect of what I might discover and create today — what ideas I might hunt and catch. This gives me a genuine sense of purpose.

Every blank page in my notebook is new terrain to explore. Anything could happen. At any moment I could stumble across a sentence that will be remembered and quoted in a hundred years. This is the thrill of the creative process. We never know what ideas are waiting to be discovered around the corner. The hunting instinct is activated, giving our lives a sense of mystery and meaning.

The law of creative abundance.

There is a pesky and lingering fear inside me that one day I will run out of ideas. The well will dry up. I'll sit down to write and nothing will happen. "Thanks for playing," the muse will say. "Now go get a real job."

Luckily, I am always proven wrong. An emotion will spark a new idea, a random thought will jump into my head. A new experience leads to a new perspective. There are limitless variations to the human condition and therefore limitless variations to art.

"You can't use up creativity.

The more you use, the more you have."

MAYA ANGELOU

Creativity, it turns out, isn't a well that can dry up. It's an ocean that is perpetually renewed. Ideas are not a limited resource. Like sunlight or oxygen, the regenerative energy of creation is a gift in endless supply. After all, creativity isn't generated with force or effort. It is a universal energy that we tap into and receive like the organic spirit of nature itself.

I'm often amazed to think about how long humans have been making music, yet new songs are created each year that sound nothing like the music that came before. Every piano has the same eighty-eight keys, but on any given day a musician can sit down and play a specific combination of notes that has never been played before. The possible arrangement of letters and words into sequences to denote meaning are infinite. This specific sentence I'm writing now has never been written before and will never be written again. Even if you have a similar idea to somebody else—ideas are never owned, merely borrowed—nobody else can express it exactly the way you can.

We live in an abundant universe. Everything we need to survive and thrive—our bodies, water, sunlight, food, air, fire, beauty—is given to us freely. Nature provides. The only constraints on our abundance are the socially constructed regulations that attempt to limit and control the natural flow of energy and resources. When it comes to creativity, these socially constructed regulations come in the form of ego, doubt, overthinking, and other mental blocks.

Creativity is natural. Being stuck is unnatural. But we need to keep showing up with dedication so the muse knows she can trust us with her secrets. We need to keep the energy flowing, purging the mind again and again to make room for new ideas. Receive, express, receive, express, repeat. Like breathing.

Get started now. Don't worry about being perfect. Don't worry about running out of ideas. Make your creative practice a habit, a ritual. Show up whether you feel like it or not. Just like a romantic relationship, what you get out of the creative process is equal to the effort you put in.

Develop a ritual

A ritual is any habit done with sacred intention. When you treat your creative process like a sacred ritual, you are cultivating a presence of mind and inviting the muse to join you. No two creative processes look alike. Find a routine that works for you. The following are some steps to take when developing your ritual.

1. Create a sacred space

Choose a room or nook in a room and designate it for creativity. Keep it as clean and organized as possible. A clean room helps us think clearly. Treat your ritual like a ceremony. The composer Terry Riley takes off his shoes before entering his studio, as if it were a temple. Take your time, light a candle or incense, play instrumental music, bring your favorite beverage, and get into a meditative state of mind.

2. Choose a dedicated time

It helps to choose a specific time each day, a time when your mind is fresh and you won't be disturbed. It's important to have blocks of uninterrupted time during the creative process. For me, mornings are best, before the demands and distractions of the day start knocking on my door. Set a reminder or alarm on your phone to help get you in a groove.

3. Thirty days of creation

Make a commitment to spend thirty consecutive days doing something creative. You can either pick a single project or experiment with different ideas. It could be learning an instrument, working on poetry, developing a business plan, or launching a podcast—whatever you feel called to create. Show up consistently for thirty days. Don't worry about the quality or quantity of production, and certain days will be easier than others. The point is to keep showing up, making the creative process a ritual. Repetition makes habits.

STAGES OF
CREATIVE MASTERY

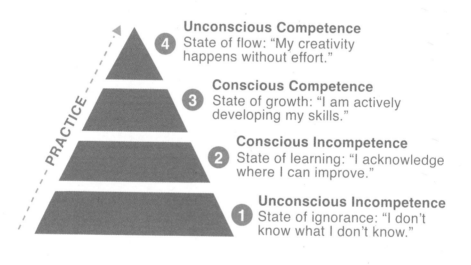

Unconscious Competence
4 State of flow: "My creativity happens without effort."

Conscious Competence
3 State of growth: "I am actively developing my skills."

Conscious Incompetence
2 State of learning: "I acknowledge where I can improve."

Unconscious Incompetence
1 State of ignorance: "I don't know what I don't know."

PRACTICE

CHANGE IS NATURAL

NATURE IS NEVER STATIC. IT IS ALWAYS CHANGING, DYING, AND BEING REBORN. THE SEASONS ARE IN CONSTANT TRANSITION.

THE NATURE OF THE ARTIST IS ALSO TO CHANGE. TO GROW AND EVOLVE. TO REINVENT OURSELVES. TO SHED OUR WORN OUT SKIN.

THE HUMAN SPIRIT (LIKE THE CYCLE OF WATER) IS NOT MEANT TO BE STAGNANT. IT'S MEANT TO BREATHE. TO RAIN. TO EVAPORATE AND REAPPEAR IN NEW FORMS.

IT'S NEVER TOO LATE TO CHANGE. DON'T HOLD ONTO THE WAY THINGS USED TO BE. GIVE YOURSELF PERMISSION TO BECOME SOMEBODY NEW.

Chapter 11

EXPERIMENTATION AND PLAY

"There are no right answers for anything involved in art.
We're all trying experiments to find a way. I don't have a set
way that I do anything. I come to every project blank."

RICK RUBIN

MAKING ART IS a process of discovery. You might have an idea in your head—a desired destination—but exactly how you'll get there remains a mystery. Every work of art is a new invention, and invention begins with experimentation and play. Even if the subject matter is serious, the process of creation is never serious. The process is about curiosity and exploration— trying something to see what happens. Like a child playing a game of make believe, we invent the path as we go. Creativity is intelligence having fun.

Like scientists working in a lab, you need to try different experiments to find a breakthrough. Not all experiments work, but through trial and error, they get closer and closer to a solution.

The definition of "experiment" is to test a hypothesis by purposefully trying something new without attachment to specific results. All creation is a series of experiments, repeatedly asking, "What if?" *What if*

I play these notes together? What if I add this color? What if I use this metaphor? What if I test a new app feature? What if I introduce a new product to the market? None of these questions has a right or wrong answer. Each is merely an experiment, an artistic game of make-believe. If you don't like the result, try something else.

An experiment is a deviation from the norm, trying something you haven't done before. This could be a new technique, new genre, or new subject matter. Experimentation keeps our work fresh and infuses it with new energy. If we keep doing the same thing over and over again, we'll keep getting the same results. If we want to reach a new destination, we must be willing to sail off into the unknown and lose sight of the shore.

Challenging convention.

One of my favorite examples of fearless experimentation is the music of David Bowie, who pushed rock 'n' roll into new territory. As a young man, Bowie was fascinated by theater. He dreamt of one day writing and producing his own plays but had no idea where to start. Instead, he started writing music and conceiving theatrical stories in songs and albums.

After adopting the persona of a psychedelic folk singer and making bold decisions such as wearing a dress on an album cover, Bowie took a huge creative leap in 1972 with the release of his breakthrough album *The Rise and Fall of Ziggy Stardust and the Spiders from Mars*. More than just an album, Ziggy Stardust was a persona that Bowie invented—an alien rock star who had landed on Earth to save the planet from impending doom. Bowie acted out the character on stage, draped in glittery alien regalia. It was like nothing the world of music had seen before.

Ziggy Stardust was a huge success, bringing Bowie critical acclaim and worldwide fame, but the character didn't last long. It was merely the first of many reinventions Bowie would make in his career. By 1973, he had already moved on to his next alter ego, Aladdin Sane. He would never perform as Ziggy Stardust again.

Throughout his long career as a songwriter and musician, Bowie consistently reinvented himself in bold and daring ways, shapeshifting from one genre and one character to the next. He wasn't chasing trends; he was inventing them. His recording studio was a science lab where he dissected rock 'n' roll and experimented with new sounds and visions, inspiring new musical genres like glam rock, punk, and new wave.

"If you feel safe in the area you're working in, you're not working in the right area," Bowie said. "Always go a little further into the water than you feel you're capable of being in. Go a little bit out of your depth. And when you don't feel that your feet are quite touching the bottom, you're just about in the right place to do something exciting."

Another example of bold experimentation comes from the writer William S. Burroughs, a member of the Beat Generation literary movement. His first two novels, *Junkie* and *Queer*, dealt with subject matters (drugs and homosexuality) that were quite taboo in 1950s America. By experimenting beyond acceptable literary topics, Burroughs broke down the door for other writers to express their own truths, even when those truths were uncomfortable.

"In my writing I am acting as a mapmaker, an explorer of psychic areas, a cosmonaut of inner space, and I see no point in exploring areas that have already been thoroughly surveyed."

WILLIAM S. BURROUGHS

Although *Junkie* and *Queer* were shocking in their subject matter, stylistically they were still conventional. Burroughs's stylistic experimentations began with his third novel, *Naked Lunch*. After spending time with the visual artist Brion Gysin, Burroughs was inspired to bring the art of collage—a visual technique of juxtaposing various often-unrelated images together—into his writing. He developed a technique he called the "cut-up method," in which he took various pieces he'd written, along with other "found" material such as newspaper clippings, and he cut up the text with a scissors. He then rearranged the text—a few words here, a few sentences there—in strange and unexpected ways.

Burroughs's intention was to use the cut-up method to break literature free from the confines of linear thought to add an element of randomness and chance. The resulting text is often difficult to understand, but it was a stylistic breakthrough in the world of literature, giving other writers permission to fearlessly experiment with technique.

Experimenting with technology.

Art and language are always changing and evolving. From the hieroglyphic stone engravings in ancient Egypt to the handwritten letters of the Victorian Era to the instant text messages we send today, each generation expresses itself through the tools and technology of its time.

Artistic innovation is often driven by the adoption of new technology. When technology is new, it seems like a novelty or a gimmick rather than a serious creative medium. But through a series of experiments by early adopters, new technology eventually becomes understood and accepted as a legitimate channel of creative expression.

The art that comes to define each generation is made with the commonplace tools and technology of its time. Examples include the silkscreen painting of Andy Warhol, the spray-paint graffiti of Jean-Michel Basquiat, or the turntable scratching of early hip-hop music. In the moment it might not appear to be art, but in hindsight it is obviously recognized as such.

Today, the internet is a town square where art and ideas are created and shared. Our commonplace tools are smartphones, social media, and emerging technologies like artificial intelligence (AI) and virtual reality (VR). These tools are the next artistic frontier, and they provide a new playground of creative expression.

In recent years, artificial intelligence has advanced at a rapid pace, causing both celebration and concern. With a simple human prompt, AI algorithms can produce written, visual, or video content with a shocking degree of fidelity. Though this is amazing from a technological perspective, some people have disparaged the diminishing human role in the creation of art. Personally, I don't see AI art as a replacement for human art. I see AI as another tool for humans to utilize in the process of bringing their visions to life, much like computers. Computers have changed the way we live and work, eliminating some jobs while creating other, unforeseen jobs.

The creative human spirit cannot be replaced by technology. Tools such as AI and VR create a wider cosmic canvas in which innovative artists can experiment and play. Creative expression is always evolving. Art finds a way.

Meme magic: Art in the age of social media.

At the end of 2019, my girlfriend and I left New York City and relocated to Topanga Canyon, on the outskirts of Los Angeles, exchanging the crowded subway for the healing saltwater of the Pacific Ocean. At the time, I was working on a novel. It was my first time writing fiction. Every single morning, I sat down at my computer and typed. When it came time to pitch to publishers, however, the book was rejected by every single one. The publishing industry, I learned, doesn't like it when an author switches genres. "You're not known as a fiction writer," was the consensus opinion. "You'd better stick to nonfiction."

I was devastated. I had already spent hundreds of hours writing the book and nobody wanted to publish it. It felt frustrating to have the means of content distribution outside my control. Thinking of how I could share my writing and art with an audience without the need of an institutional gatekeeper, I considered social media. Was it possible, I wondered, to devote my creative energy to making art designed specifically for social media, the same way someone might write a book or make a painting? What would this sort of internet art look like?

We had been living in California for only a few months before the COVID-19 pandemic began. Nearly overnight, the world was thrown into chaos. To minimize the spread of the virus, a global quarantine was enforced. Businesses shut down. Even the hiking trails in Topanga were closed.

One day, while flipping through an art book, I stumbled across the Dada movement of the early twentieth century, which began as a response to World War I, a time of unprecedented change in Europe. As both a literary and art movement, Dada often blended the two together to form striking (and sometimes silly) visual poetry. *Weird times call for weird art*, I thought. The Dada artists combined visuals and language in strange ways to communicate the strangeness of their times. For example, the French painter Marcel Duchamp once placed an actual urinal in a museum and called it art. Even the word *Dada* was random. An artist opened a German dictionary to a random page and pointed to a random word. The name *Dada*, which originally referred to a toy horse, went on to define the creative movement.

I couldn't help but make at least some connection between the early days of World War I and the early days of COVID. Both were times of death, confusion, and rapid change. Not only was a pandemic creeping its way across the world, much of the economy had been shut down. Depression and suicide were at all-time highs. Spreading just as quickly as COVID-19 were conspiracy theories about the virus. Where had it originated? Was it part of a plan to enforce authoritarian control? The world felt eerie and uncertain. Following the tragic killing of George

Floyd by a police officer in Minneapolis, riots and protests began popping up all over the country. Buildings were set on fire, and stores were looted. The social fabric of the United States was quickly unraveling, leaving people scrambling to make sense of it all.

With nowhere to go, I started spending more time than ever on the internet, refreshing Twitter and falling down esoteric YouTube rabbit holes. One evening I found myself watching an interview with the psychedelic philosopher Terence McKenna. He was talking about the power of memes to communicate ideas. "Our task is to create memes," he said. "Launch your meme boldly and see if it will replicate."

Memes? I thought. *Aren't memes those funny images with captions that people share on social media? Why was Terence McKenna talking about memes back in the 1990s, when the internet was still in its infancy?*

I started doing some research. The word *meme*, I learned, was coined in 1976 by evolutionary biologist Richard Dawkins in his book *The Selfish Gene*. The term was adapted from the Greek *mimema*, which means "imitated." A meme, Dawkins explained, is a unit of cultural information spread by imitation—*a viral idea*. What a gene is to biology, a meme is to culture. In other words, the way a gene can mutate, adapt, and cause systemic change within a biological system, a meme can take root in the mind of an individual and be passed to others, who pass it along, creating a network effect of influence.

Memes and genes have the same goal: to replicate. The success of each is determined by how far they spread. A highly successful gene can permanently modify its host environment. A successful meme can permanently change a culture. A meme can come in any number of forms. A slogan such as "Make love, not war" is a meme. A fashion trend is a meme. Patriotism is a meme. Communism is a meme. A dance trend is a meme. Propaganda is a weaponized meme. Terence McKenna described a meme as the smallest unit of an idea that still has coherency.

Memes took on new life with the emergence of the internet. Never before could ideas spread so far so quickly. As the internet evolved, so did its language. New forms of expression emerged, including acronyms, emojis, and GIFs. Meanwhile, the sharing functionality of social media helped this language spread faster than any language in history. Here is where Richard Dawkins's original concept of memetics joined forces with the emerging internet language to give birth to a new art form: the internet meme.

An internet meme could be any idea that goes viral online, especially an idea that sparks imitation. This could include anything from social media challenges (planking, the Ice Bucket Challenge) to a linguistic Twitter trend ("said no one ever") to a visual that's adapted for multiple purposes (Crying Jordan) to a TikTok dance craze.

A good way to understand memes is to compare them to another internet phenomenon: the emoji. An emoji is a cartoon icon that can be used to replace or accentuate words. Not only does an emoji represent an object, activity, or feeling, it does so with a visual flair that emotionally enhances the message. In this sense, an emoji communicates more than what the icon represents. The emotional tone of the emoji is just as important. Memes are the same. Because of the humorous and unexpected way in which they deliver a message, they add an emotional subtext to a topic that would be difficult to render with regular speech.

The internet meme has proven to be a fun and effective form of art and communication. Memes spread around the world faster than any artform in history. They spark a visceral reaction that compels people to share. The right combination of image and text can communicate an idea or emotion better—and more quickly—than several long paragraphs.

While studying the science of memetics, the idea struck me to adopt the internet meme as a format of creative expression. What would poetry, spirituality, and philosophy look like, I wondered, filtered through the quirky style of internet memes? Inspired by the apocalyptic state of the world, the Dada movement, and Terence McKenna, I began to experiment with writing that was absurd, funny, easily consumed, ironic, and existential—*writing that spoke the native language of the internet.*

Instead of waking up each morning to work on my books, I started putting my creative energy toward social media content, allowing me to share my work with an audience on a regular basis. I quickly realized that memes could be a potent tool of creativity and communication. The combination of image/caption added a whole new dimension to my writing process. I could suddenly express things, including the strangeness of the world, that I hadn't been able to fully express before.

Memes felt more "now" than other types of writing, more immediate and relevant to the world I was living in. They also turned out to be quite popular. Within a matter of months, my social media following doubled, then tripled, then quadrupled. Growing a social media following is largely based on how many people share and engage with your content. Easily digestible memes, which also provided a hit of deeper meaning, proved to be something that people loved sharing.

I learned to adapt my writing to fit the very short format. Like the art of the Japanese haiku, I had to limit my words to the absolute essential. I experimented with making memes in different ways, using various design tools. Sometimes I would discover a funny image and try to think of a caption. Sometimes it was the other way around: I would think of something I wanted to say, then look for an image to articulate the sentiment. Like all forms of creativity, mastering the craft of memes requires experimentation and trial and error.

My journey of making memes culminated in 2021 when I released my second book, *How to Laugh in Ironic Amusement During Your Existential Crisis*, a hopeful and humorous collection of poetry and memes inspired by an upside-down world. It was the first published book of memes.

In case of emergency, break routine.

When we try something new, our brains light up with stimulation, widening our access to a broader neural network. But after a while, the novelty wears off. The neural pathways we forge become stale and routine. What once brought excitement now feels boring.

> "If you think adventure is dangerous,
>
> try routine — it is lethal."

PAULO COELHO

Neuro-linguistic programming (NLP) teaches a practice called "pattern interruption." Interrupting your pattern means altering a mental or behavioral state by introducing a random or unexpected element. For example, think of how drastically your daily routine would be interrupted if you were suddenly transported to a foreign country where you don't speak the language. With no default state to fall back on, you would have no choice but to experiment and explore.

Interrupting your creative process on a regular basis is a great way to stay fresh and inspired. If you're feeling stuck, try something new. Experiment with form or technique. Try a different genre or creative medium. Step outside your normal process and do something that makes you uncomfortable. Art has no right or wrong answers, no predetermined path. Like life itself, we make it up as we go: trying, failing, experimenting, and learning lessons along the way. The deeper we explore, the more we discover.

Think of yourself as a scientist in a lab. You're not aiming for perfection or trying to copy somebody else. You're simply testing ideas and mixing chemicals together to see what happens. Art is an artifact left over from the trial and error of experimentation.

What if . . . ?

We expand as people and creators when we stretch ourselves beyond our comfort zone. In our lives and art, we are often following arbitrary rules and traditions that have been handed down to us. The best ideas in art, business, science, and technology start by questioning the prevailing status quo.

For this exercise, make a list of ten different "what ifs" related to your life, your career, and your art. For example:

- What if I changed my name?

- What if I tried drawing with my nondominant hand?

- What if I wrote a poem from the perspective of an alien?

- What if I tried to meet a new person every day for a week?

- What if I monetized one of my hobbies?

The point is to disrupt your perception of what is normal and acceptable. No "what if" is too outlandish. Be as random and far out as possible.

TRY

LOOKING

FROM

A DIFFERENT

PERSPECTIVE

NO

ARTIST

TOLERATES

REALITY

— Friedrich Nietzsche

Chapter 12

LAUNCHING YOUR WORK

UP UNTIL NOW, the creative process has been a mostly solitary endeavor. The nurturing and development of ideas happens primarily behind closed doors, inside the mind of the creator and close collaborators. This safe, uninterrupted womb is necessary for creativity to incubate and bloom. The muse is like a gentle bluebird, easily startled by too much attention. It's best to let your ideas gestate until they are strong enough to survive and thrive on their own. But sooner or later, you have to give birth. Your ideas must graduate from the privacy of your mind and take their place on the public stage. This is the natural conclusion of the creative process: to launch, to be known and seen.

Launching comes in all shapes and sizes. Perhaps you are starting a business, a podcast, an online course, a book, or a YouTube show. Launching could mean posting content on social media. Whether big or small, launching can be an anxiety-inducing prospect. When I help my clients develop creative projects, going public is often the most challenging step. The naked exposure of making the private world public can feel vulnerable and embarrassing. What if nobody likes it? Even worse, what if nobody cares?

Never compare your audience or acclaim to anyone else's. Everyone is at a different phase in their personal and artistic journey. Have patience with yourself as you forge your own path. What's important is to launch your work so you can release it from your system, to make room for the next idea, and to gather feedback (good or bad) that you can use as you continue to experiment and grow.

Editing.

The creation process is like filling your home with furniture, decorations, and other belongings. The content is there. But it needs to be sorted, organized, and arranged. Certain things need to be placed in certain rooms. You might have too many forks but not enough spoons. Editing is how you take what you have and craft it into something complete.

There is a difference between expression and craftsmanship. Expression is a calling from the soul, a release of something that wants to come out. Craftsmanship is more mental—a time to review, analyze, add, subtract, and rearrange. This is where your inner critic finally gets its chance to shine.

Editing is about distilling your work down to its essence and removing anything unnecessary. What is essential? What is the main point? Remove or change anything that distracts from the essence. A good rule of thumb is to err on the side of simplicity. The fashion designer Coco Chanel said that it's always better to be underdressed than overdressed. Her rule of thumb for leaving the house was to look in the mirror and take one thing off.

It's a good idea to fact-check your instincts with a critical eye. Instincts are good at big-picture ideas, but not always great with details. Once I've completed a good chunk of writing, I go back, review, and make changes as necessary. My philosophy is simple: make every sentence strong. While editing, I don't worry about the entire book. I only focus on one sentence at a time. It's about balancing the right and left sides of the brain, the imaginative and the logical. When you're making something, let it flow without censorship. But when it's time to edit, be critical—within reason—of your own conclusions. Create without fear; edit without mercy.

Launch before you're ready.

Launching is about finishing your work and making it available for the world to see. That doesn't mean it's perfect. The pursuit of perfection is an excuse not to launch. All art is a snapshot of a moment in time. Could it be different? Sure. Could it be better? Maybe. But at a certain point the bird needs to fly away from the nest.

In the business and technology world, there is a concept called MVP: minimum viable product. The point of the MVP is to get to market as soon as possible, before the product is finished, in order to build awareness and collect feedback. A digital product like an app or website is never considered finished, but rather in a state of constant iteration. The point is to be agile, growing and adapting over time according to the needs of the customer. We learn best by doing.

I launched my podcast in 2019. Was I ready? Not exactly. I've always been comfortable sharing the written word. The spoken-word format of podcasting—not so much. I knew there would be a learning curve, that it would take me a while to get my footing. But I knew that it would be impossible to improve without starting. So I decided to launch right away, before I was ready. I wanted to get the bad episodes out of the way so I could start recording good ones.

As expected, it wasn't an immediate success. I didn't have the right equipment. My interview style was forced and uptight. I even changed the podcast name three times within the first two years. But I learned an important lesson: you can't improve what you don't start. Launching before I was ready gave me a sandbox in which to practice.

Don't hold onto your art too tightly. It wants to be set free. Sharing is an important stage in the creative process, a release of the energy you are nurturing. Remember that it's only an expression of the present moment. Lower the stakes. Launch and move on. Keep the momentum going.

How often to launch.

In the mid-1960s during the rock 'n' roll revolution, artists were launching albums at a rapid pace. In just two years (1965 and 1966) Bob Dylan released three classic albums that would change the face of music and literature for years to come. Dylan wrote, recorded, and launched quickly, completing a final song in just one or two takes. He didn't overthink his music. And the lively spirit of spontaneous energy is still palpable in the recordings.

The Beatles were just as prolific. The band's entire legendary run of recorded music happened in just seven years (1963–1970) when they released nearly two albums each year. (They also released five movies during that time.) Each subsequent album took on a new shape and a new sound, and the band kept moving forward without looking back.

Other artists work at a slower pace, treating each launch as a special event. The singer Frank Ocean releases an album roughly every five years and remains relatively out of the public spotlight between launches. Some say that Frank is doing his career a disservice by making himself scarce, that he would be more famous and wealthy if he released new music on a more frequent basis. But Frank is playing a longer game. In a world saturated with information, music, and content, his music remains a luxury. Each release feels special. And because he doesn't overexpose himself, Frank doesn't wear out his welcome. He leaves his fans wanting more.

The way people produce and consume content has changed significantly in recent years. New media platforms like podcasting and YouTube have normalized a more frequent cadence of launching content. Dedicated podcasters release a new episode every week. Many YouTubers release a video every single day. In this new paradigm, it's not about making perfect art. It's about being a regular and reliable presence in the lives of the audience.

Quality and quantity are both important. Don't hold your art too tightly, but also don't force it. Don't withhold, but also don't overshare. Wait until you have a statement to make, then launch with conviction.

Posting on social media.

These days, much of our public sharing (artistic or otherwise) happens on social media. This is the new town square, the place where we gather, exchange ideas, and promote ourselves. When it comes to launching our work, social media can be used both to announce and promote a project, such as an event or a book, and as a creative medium unto itself. Art that is native to social media—such as videos, short-form writing, and memes—is some of the most engaging and impactful art being created today.

I used to think that social media content was frivolous and shallow—a passing fad, not real art. But I've gradually changed my perspective. A single meme might not have the same impact as reading a novel or watching a movie, but a book or a film is typically a one-time thing. You finish it and move on. Some of the information is retained; some is forgotten. But if you follow somebody on social media for three years and that person shares every single day, then their thoughts become a regular part of your life.

In the language of psychedelics, this is like microdosing art. You might not have a hugely significant experience from just one post, but a little hit each day, over the course of months or years, can reorient your entire life. Social media content, when done well, can be real art. It's just released and consumed differently.

Of course, social media is not without downsides. As digital products, they are designed to be highly addictive, rewarding us with tiny hits of dopamine so we keep crawling back. The effects on mental health have been well documented, and the findings are not promising, especially on young people.

I was recently invited to give a talk at Meta (the company behind social media platforms Facebook and Instagram) on the topic of memes, mindfulness, and creativity. The talk was hosted by Meta's Mindfulness Club, who call themselves "the mystics in the machine" and try to plant seeds of awareness into the collective mind of the tech giant. God bless them.

Social media gives us tremendous power. It also holds tremendous power over us. It's important that we use these tools with purpose and intention instead of being mindlessly sucked into the screen's bright and shiny vortex. In my talk, I stressed the importance of using social media for creation and education rather than mere consumption. Our relationship to social media improves drastically when we use it to create, experiment, and express ourselves, rather than passively scrolling through an endless, disempowering sea of content.

Personally, I think of my iPhone as a portable art studio. My Notes app is a sketchbook where I jot down ideas. My Camera Roll is storage for source material. And Instagram and Twitter are my art galleries and broadcast channels where I share my ideas. When I'm scrolling, I'm generally looking for inspiration to fuel my own content.

Posting content on social media can sometimes feel like a chore. We live in a world that is increasingly public. It feels like we are expected to be "on" 24/7, broadcasting our lives for the world to see. In such a huge ocean of content—swimming with memes, sexually suggestive content, and funny cat videos—does anyone really care about what you have to say? Will it make any difference?

I'm an introvert by nature. Sharing myself openly on a regular basis, especially on video, doesn't come naturally to me. It feels cringe to be overexposed. Sometimes I would rather retreat to a mountaintop to meditate in silence, far away from Wi-Fi access. But I gradually learned to reframe my relationship to social media. I'm not performing, I decided. I'm not trying to put on a show or be anyone I'm not. My audience isn't even an audience. They are casual friends, and I'm merely opening my door to invite them inside. If the house is a little messy, so be it. I intentionally share my flaws and insecurities as much as my highlights. After all, real life isn't a highlight reel. It's a full spectrum of ups and downs. I'd rather be imperfectly honest than insincerely perfect.

The irony is that when we put down our guard and share our genuine, imperfect selves, we forge a deeper connection with our audience. People are starving for authenticity. Imperfections are relatable. They make us seem less packaged, more human. When we share our authentic selves, we give others permission to do the same, to accept their whole being, warts and all, instead of striving for unrealistic expectations.

Dealing with negative feedback.

When our work is private, it is safe and protected. But as soon as we launch, we open ourselves to criticism. This comes with the territory of working in public. It doesn't matter how talented, smart, or compassionate you are. All artists and creators are a target for a certain degree of negative feedback. The bigger your audience, the more criticism. It's a universal law.

People are often challenged when faced with art that is new and different. The default reaction is to be dismissive. Even established artists are not immune. Early in his career, Bob Dylan was a traditional folk singer. He played acoustic guitar and sang in the rootsy, plainspoken style of his childhood hero, Woody Guthrie. But Dylan had a secret love for rock 'n' roll music, which was new, exciting, and electric. He also wanted to experiment with songwriting that was more like modern poetry: abstract, psychedelic, and surreal.

Dylan debuted his new sound at the Newport Folk Festival in 1965, where he publicly played an electric guitar for the first time. The audience was furious. At the time, rock 'n' roll music was still considered a silly novelty by some, not like the serious folk music they had come to see. Dylan was booed by the crowd. Someone even shouted "Judas," implying that Dylan was a traitor. But Dylan had conviction in his new style despite the negative feedback. He turned to his electric band, shouted over the booing audience, and instructed them to "play it fucking loud."

Listening to feedback from the crowd can sometimes be helpful, but sometimes it's a distraction from our vision and purpose. It's important to use discernment when listening to criticism. When you have conviction in your own intuition, don't lose your focus by pandering to other people's opinions. Your inner wisdom knows which form your art should take. Only a few months after being booed at the Newport Folk Festival, Bob Dylan's folk-infused electric music and psychedelic lyrics would make him one of the most popular musicians in the world.

If your work receives negative feedback, congratulations, you are part of a large and prestigious club. Even some of the best and most enduring works of art were criticized upon launch. Don't believe me? Take a look at the following reviews.

Abbey Road by The Beatles

"An unmitigated disaster." —The *New York Times*, 1969

Lolita by Vladmir Nabokov

"Lolita, then, is undeniably news in the world of books. Unfortunately, it is bad news. There are two equally serious reasons why it isn't worth any adult reader's attention. The first is that it is dull, dull, dull in a pretentious, florid and archly fatuous fashion. The second is that it is repulsive." —The *New York Times*, 1958

Anna Karenina by Leo Tolstoy

"Sentimental rubbish . . . Show me one page that contains an idea." —*The Odessa Courier*, 1877

Kid A by Radiohead

"It is the sound of Thom Yorke ramming his head firmly up his own arse, hearing the rumblings of his intestinal wind, and deciding to share it with the world." —*Melody Maker*, 2000

Ulysses by James Joyce

". . . appears written by a perverted lunatic who has made a speciality of the literature of the latrine . . . Two-thirds of it is incoherent, and the passages that are plainly written are devoid of wit." — *The Sporting Times*, 1922

The Godfather: Part II directed by Francis Ford Coppola

"Everything of any interest was thoroughly covered in the original film, but like many people who have nothing to say, Part II won't shut up." —The *New York Times,* 1974

Initial iPhone launch by Apple

"The iPhone will be a major disappointment." —*Advertising Age*, 2007

It's important to remember that opinions are merely that: opinions. Everyone has one. None are objectively true. Some people are predisposed to seek out what they *don't* like about something rather than what they *do* like. And negative voices always shout louder than positive ones. Whatever you do, don't take it personally. Criticism usually says more about the critic than it does about the art.

Posting on social media opens us up to all sorts of criticism and misinterpretation. Nearly everything I share gets at least a few negative comments. This used to bother me. I took it as an assault on my talent and intelligence. I might get a hundred positive comments and a single negative comment, yet the negative comment would stand out.

Over time I learned not to take criticism personally. In fact, it can be helpful. Generally speaking, criticism can be divided into two categories. The first is challenging your point of view with another perspective. This is helpful feedback. We all have biases and blind spots. Listening to other perspectives has made me a better writer because it has helped me add more thoughtful nuance to my language, making my work more inclusive and accessible.

The other category of criticism is unhelpful, mean spirited, and rude. Perhaps the critical person completely misunderstands what you are saying, and they're projecting their own, skewed interpretation. This sort of feedback doesn't aim to educate or add nuance. The critic is merely throwing rocks, trying to extend the anger and hurt within themselves. It's easy to be triggered by these sorts of destructive comments, but I do my best (it's not always easy!) to witness them through a lens of compassion. There are many people who are isolated or living with chronic emotional pain. They might not mean to be rude, but they're reacting impulsively without truly considering the human on the other side of the screen.

Social media lowers the barrier of criticism and insults. People will type a comment that they would never dream of speaking in real life. In other words, it is not the real world, but often a place of half-conscious reactivity. It's best not to dwell on the negative comments. And if they are especially toxic, don't hesitate to delete and block. Protect your mind. Protect your energy. Move on.

Preparing for liftoff.

In my work as a brand strategist, I helped many companies launch. While no business or project is ever completely final, it does help to launch with your best foot forward. Following is a checklist to consider while preparing to launch a project.

1. Naming

What are you (or your business or project) known as? What is your social media handle and website address? Your podcast name? Many creatives use their birth name. Others invent their own identity. I randomly chose the Instagram name @wordsarevibrations, and it stuck. When thinking of a name, aim for simplicity—something that is easy to remember and will age well. It's more important for a name to be memorable than to describe exactly what you do. .

2. Mission statement

A mission statement is a clear and concise description—usually a paragraph—of what you do and the impact you hope to make on the world. This can be written for yourself as a creator, for your business, or for a project. A mission statement provides clarity and a sense of purpose, a North Star to follow.

3. Tagline/bio

If you had to summarize yourself, your business, or your project in one sentence, what would it be? A tagline or social media bio is a simple and catchy distillation of who you are and what you offer. For example, instead of labeling myself as an "author" or "artist," my Instagram bio used to say "post-apocalyptic psychedelic meme poet." It was a funny and memorable way to carve out a niche that was wholly my own.

4. Visual aesthetic

My former career as a graphic designer taught me the importance of developing a consistent visual language. Things to consider: logo, color palette, typography, and photography. I usually start the design process by creating a moodboard, which is a collection of images and graphics that articulate the style and mood I'm going for.

5. Audience personas

It helps to have a clear idea about who your audience will be. What is their age, gender, income, and lifestyle? What challenges are they facing, and how does your work support them? When you have a clear idea about who your project is serving, you'll have a better idea about how you can connect with them.

Validate yourself.

In the past, the modes of creative production and distribution were largely out of the creator's hands. Artists relied on institutional gatekeepers to validate and launch their work. In order to be read, heard, or seen, an artist needed to be anointed by a publisher, a record label, financial investors, or a gallery owner, who served as a liaison between the art and the audience.

Luckily, this is changing. The rise of decentralized technology platforms like social media, podcasts, and YouTube has made it easier for artists to launch their work and grow an audience without institutional support. The power dynamic is shifting. Now, anyone anywhere, regardless of their formal education or industry connections, can launch their art into the marketplace of ideas and, if it resonates, make a name for themselves.

The key is authenticity. If you want to make deep connections with your audience, your work needs to come from deep inside yourself. You must explore your inner and outer worlds and funnel your pain, joy, sadness, and love into your art, like a map of your personal journey.

As the world continues to change and the old power structures continue to atrophy, there is a vacancy for true leaders, problem solvers, healers, artists, and dreamers. Don't wait for institutional permission or validation. Validate yourself. Launch your work. Offer your vision as medicine for the world.

Celebrate yourself

When we launch a project, whether big or small, we get it out of our system. The baby bird leaves the nest to begin a life of its own. We can't control how our work is received or perceived by others, so it's best to drop expectations. Let go with gratitude.

It doesn't matter if your project is seen by millions of people or only a few. Like giving birth, your launch is a cause for celebration. Give yourself time to appreciate the moment. Make an announcement. Celebrate with friends. Commemorate the moment before moving on. You deserve it.

HOW TO
DEVELOP YOUR PROJECT
(Start big picture, then gradually zoom in)

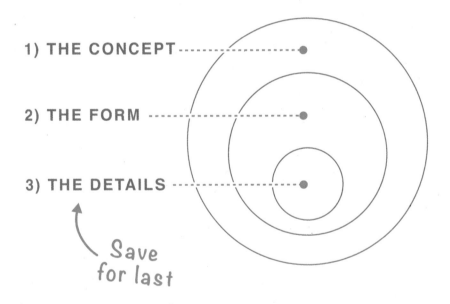

1) THE CONCEPT

2) THE FORM

3) THE DETAILS

Save
for last

RULES FOR CREATIVE BALANCE

FEEL YOUR FEELINGS BUT DON'T GET STUCK THERE

LET YOUR MIND WANDER BUT BRING YOUR VISION BACK TO EARTH

USE YOUR INTELLIGENCE BUT DON'T OVERANALYZE

BE PRODUCTIVE BUT GIVE YOURSELF SPACE TO REST

EDIT BUT DON'T OBSESS ABOUT PERFECTION

SHARE YOUR WORK BUT RELEASE ATTACHMENT TO THE RESULTS

Chapter 13

GOING PRO

"Your work is going to fill a large part of your life, and the only way to be truly satisfied is to do what you believe is great work. And the only way to do great work is to love what you do. If you haven't found it yet, keep looking. Don't settle. As with all matters of the heart, you'll know when you find it."

STEVE JOBS

MAKING ART IS one thing. Making a career out of creativity is another thing entirely. We can create whenever and wherever we choose, but that doesn't necessarily mean we'll be paid for our efforts. A monetary reward is not the only—or even the biggest—incentive for creative expression. Creativity liberates our souls and restores a sense of magic to life. It is rewarding, financially or not. But still, there is great value to creative thinking. It can change lives, transform a business, and make a positive impact on society. Creative people deserve to make a good living.

The good news is that, contrary to popular opinion, creativity and wealth are not in conflict. When it comes to income generation, creativity is a valuable asset, especially in our rapidly shifting and uncertain economy. The key is knowing where and how to direct our creative energy.

The myth of the starving artist.

There is an archetype perpetuated by society of the broke, hapless artist passionately writing or painting their way directly into poverty. Artists and innovators do not make money, this myth implies. If we follow our creative urges instead of making more pragmatic career decisions, we will struggle to survive.

The patron saint of the starving artist archetype is the French painter Vincent Van Gogh, who battled mental illness and struggled to sell a single painting during his lifetime—paintings that are now universally celebrated and worth hundreds of millions of dollars. After a lonely and tumultuous life, Van Gogh committed suicide at age thirty-seven, unknown by the art world. Creative genius, this story suggests, is not appreciated while the artist is still alive.

I flirted with this archetype myself. At age nineteen, I dropped out of college to "be an artist." What sort of artist I wanted to be, I wasn't quite sure. All I knew was that I preferred painting and poetry to the rigid confines of a college campus. Lacking mentors or direction, I bounced around the country taking odd jobs (gas station clerk, telemarketer, landscaper) while developing my craft as a writer and artist.

At first it was an exciting lifestyle. I didn't have much money, but I was free (outside of my low-wage working hours) to do whatever I wanted. And I could drink as much booze and smoke as much cannabis as I pleased. I was free, but it was the freedom of a stray dog. I didn't have a master, but I also didn't have direction. I roamed from town to town, making art and generally not thinking about anyone but myself.

Within a year, I was lonely and depressed. I was writing and making art, but nobody was seeing my work, let alone buying it. I was quarantined inside my own idea of what I thought an artist was "supposed" to be. Creativity wasn't the problem. The problem was my lack of purpose. My art had no social function, and my motivation and passion began to dry up.

At the time, I was living in Syracuse, New York, and working the overnight shift stocking shelves at Target. Every morning I got back to my tiny apartment at 8:00 a.m. and started drinking beer and making art. I had no guidance, no mentors, no purpose. Something needed to change. I knew that the next five years would pass in the blink of an eye, and if I didn't change my trajectory I would likely be in the same position, working dead-end jobs while creating art in private.

Seeking guidance, I searched for art schools online. I didn't know what art school could teach me, but at least it would give me direction and community. A few weeks later I packed my belongings into my worn-down Cadillac and drove a thousand miles back to Minnesota without sleeping, where I enrolled in a Minneapolis design school.

Design school taught me how to apply creative thinking to real-world problems. It wasn't just about me—it was about using design as a social utility, often in collaboration with other students. I learned about something called "design thinking," a strategic, problem-solving methodology that uses visual diagrams to guide decision-making. Creativity, I realized, is about more than just personal expression. It's about thinking outside the box to come up with innovative and nonlinear solutions.

After college I began my professional career as a graphic designer. Professional success, I quickly learned, was not determined merely by my talent but by how well I could work within a team environment. Interpersonal relationships with both clients and coworkers were critical. So was my ability to give a presentation and speak convincingly about my work. It was also important to listen to feedback. As the designer, I was guiding the project, but I needed to consider the opinions of my clients and coworkers. It was a team effort.

My younger self had been right. Five years *did* pass in the blink of an eye, but because I changed my trajectory and found a purposeful use for my creativity, I was no longer a starving artist. I was a successful creative professional.

There are many ways that creativity can be used to make money, both in and out of a corporate setting. I'm not suggesting that all creatives who wish to make money should attend art school. I'm suggesting that they apply purpose to their creative thinking in order to make a contribution to society that will be financially rewarded. If prospective medical professionals merely sat at home and practiced medicine in private—waiting to be "discovered"—then we might be talking about the myth of the starving doctor.

Creativity is a valuable skill—a skill worth money. All forms of art do have personal, emotional, and even spiritual value, but not all forms of art hold monetary value—just like all business ideas are not profitable. This is not a criticism of the artist. It simply means they have not yet found a profitable application of their talent.

The business of creativity.

Where does money come from? We speak in terms of "making" money, which implies an act of creation, building something out of nothing. Opening a new stream of income requires ingenuity and creative thinking. Every business, just like every creative project, began as a tiny idea that offered value to the world and then was developed over time. From nothing, a channel of income was conceived, nurtured, and born.

Creativity is a transferable skill. That is, creative thinking can be applied to any number of circumstances—not just making art. It's all too easy for artists to get hung up on the format they're comfortable with (e.g., drawing or dancing) rather than investigating the underlying creative process that makes their art possible. The same ingenuity that made you good at one thing can be used to make you good at something else. Some people make money by selling their creative output. Others use creative thinking to find ways to make money. Each approach is a type of art.

No matter what career you have or want to have, creativity can help you excel. At its core, creativity is about curiosity and problem-solving, which is a valuable skill in every business. In my work as a brand strategist, I've worked with countless companies in numerous industries. All of them had one thing in common: in one way or another, they felt stale and stagnant, in need of fresh energy and a new perspective.

Creativity in business isn't about having all the answers. It's about curiosity and asking questions. While sitting in meetings, I often noticed my coworkers competing to have the best solution to a problem. They felt pressure to have an answer—any answer—and often jumped to conclusions just to make a statement. I learned that there is great value in saying, "I don't know enough to have an opinion." Instead of racing for an answer just to sound smart, I asked questions that helped guide us to the root of the problem where a more impactful answer could be found.

Growing an audience.

Creativity is its own reward. It doesn't matter if you're a world-famous singer or an amateur chef—you're an artist either way. On the other hand, art is meant to be shared and enjoyed by others. It's a two-way relationship between creator and consumer. That doesn't mean you need a huge following to be considered successful. There are many artists who produce amazing work outside the glare of the spotlight. It also doesn't mean you should conform your art to meet external preferences or expectations. The best way to connect with others is to be as real and authentic as possible.

Although you don't need to grow an audience to be considered an artist, it's a rewarding process because it expands the scope of your art from "me" to "we." A two-way conversation is more interesting than talking to yourself.

Having an audience could mean different things to different people. Perhaps it means finding customers to buy your products. It might mean having a group of close friends you can cook for. If you're a free-lance designer, your audience is your potential clients. Your audience might be the people who subscribe to your email newsletter. An important audience metric is social media following. The good news is that social media provides an opportunity for anyone to grow an audience based on the merit of their creativity.

When I first started pitching books to literary agents and publishers, everybody told me the same thing: "Your audience is too small. You need to grow your marketing platform before you're ready to publish a book." I was faced with the harsh reality that an audience comes before a publishing deal, not the other way around.

My first step was to research other authors in my field to see how they were growing and maintaining their audience. Many of them, I learned, were polished public speakers. They gave lectures and produced inspirational videos. I decided that I needed to copy what others were doing in order to achieve their level of success. So I launched a YouTube channel and started recording short, inspirational videos, adopting similar themes and talking points as other authors in my field.

On one hand, this was a good experience because it pushed me out of my comfort zone and helped build my confidence in front of a camera. On the other hand, it wasn't natural. I wasn't being authentic to my own personality. Instead of expressing my own unique voice, I was following a pre-existing template. It just wasn't me. And because my heart wasn't in it, these videos did nothing to grow my audience.

Around this time, I met with a literary agent to talk about publishing my book. Although my book proposal was rejected yet again, she passed on a valuable piece of advice about growing my audience. "Whatever you do, it's got to be believable," she said. "People can tell when you're faking it. Do whatever makes your heart sing—whatever makes you feel jazzed. Put your real personality out there. It might not be for everybody, but your enthusiasm will shine through, and the right people will find you."

I took her advice to heart and thought long and hard about what made my heart sing, what made me feel jazzed. In other words, what would I be doing if money and success were not part of the equation? What is the most honest and authentic expression of myself?

It had been a long time, I realized, since I had made art. As a kid, I was always drawing and painting. Ever since getting swept away in my advertising career, I had stopped making visual art. And for the first time, I realized how much I was missing it. *Could drawing and making art help me grow my audience as an author?* Nobody else was doing it, but maybe that was a good thing.

The next day, I bought a sketchbook and drawing pens and began making little illustrations with humorous or inspirational captions. It wasn't amazing or technically skillful art. It was simple line drawings that communicated an idea. What I was saying was not so different from what I had been saying in my (unsuccessful) YouTube videos, but now I was saying it in my own voice, my own style. Looking back, this was an early iteration of what would later become memes.

I began sharing my art on social media and receiving positive feedback. People started reposting my drawings. My audience, little by little, began to grow. My art stood out because, as simple as it was, it was different from what everybody else was doing. It didn't happen overnight, but I continued to draw and write and develop my own unique way of marketing myself.

Eventually my drawings evolved into word art and memes, which combined my love for writing and design. When I started making memes, my audience grew faster than ever. From an outside perspective, it might have looked like an overnight success, but below the surface were years of trial and error, experimentation, rejection, and finding my voice. What they say is true: *It takes years to become an overnight success.*

The following is a short list of techniques for artists of all kinds who are looking to grow their audience.

1. Think in terms of community

An audience isn't an abstract concept. They are real people with feelings, hopes, and dreams. Get to know them. Interact. Welcome them into your community with open arms. It's not about "me." It's about "we." Sometimes I close my eyes and try to tune into what my audience needs from me. Having an audience is a two-way relationship.

2. Show up consistently

I'm an introvert by nature. I dislike oversharing or feeling overexposed, but growing my audience required me to get out of my comfort zone and share my work and thoughts on a regular basis. Not only will showing up consistently help you grow an audience, it will also motivate you to keep creating and to develop your voice. Rituals become habits. Habits become reality. Make sharing yourself and your art an ongoing ritual.

3. Network and collaborate

One of the most useful strategies for me has been building genuine relationships with other creators. I support them and they support me. If I have a book coming out, I reach out to my friends with podcasts and ask to be a guest on their show. I also send free copies of the book to friends and influencers in my field. Having a network of supportive friends and creators is the best (and cheapest) advertising. That's the kind of marketing that money can't buy, but it requires seeking out and nurturing relationships.

4. Do something IRL (in real life)

These days, much of our lives happen online, but don't discount the power of real-life events. Display your art in local galleries or coffee shops. Participate in an open mic night. Join or host a local meet-up group. Sharing your energy in real life and holding space for others can't be replicated on social media. Plant seeds in your local community and create real connections with the people around you. Launching

Sunflower Club, my monthly creativity gathering, helped me grow roots and make connections after moving to Austin.

5. Be an early adopter

If you want to make money in the stock market, it's important to buy a stock before it receives widespread adoption. The same is true with growing an audience. In the early years of podcasting, for example, there was less competition, making it easy for podcasters to carve out market share. Stay ahead of the game by looking for new platforms and technologies to promote your work. While it's not productive to blindly chase each new trend that comes along, it's smart to leverage new channels that are aligned with your brand and message.

Trust divine timing.

For all things there is a season—a season to plant, a season to grow, a season to harvest. It's easy to become impatient while trying to grow your audience, but the day you plant the seed is not the day you eat the fruit. Nature needs time to run her course.

Growing an audience isn't about force. It's about attraction. At the most basic level, all things come down to energy and magnetism. What we chase will resist us. What we attract will come effortlessly. Put your best work out there, boldly and consistently, and see who shows up.

Growing an audience is similar to attracting a romantic partner. If you exhibit nervous energy and come across as desperate, you're going to scare them away. But if you accept yourself fully and bring your own unique perspective to the table with poise and confidence, your energy will be infectious and attractive.

Most people equate success to numbers. *How many followers do I have? How many likes did I get?* But growing an audience is not about chasing metrics. It's about having a message, style, or personality that draws people in. External success is a natural result of having a strong internal foundation. Focus on your message, not your metrics. Your metrics will grow in proportion to the clarity of your message.

If I had been given more success and a bigger audience earlier in my career, I wouldn't have been ready. My following grew at the exact rate I was able to handle it. It's sort of like when people with no money or financial literacy suddenly win the lottery. In nearly every case, they are unable to sustain their newfound wealth. It's only a matter of time until they are back to where they started. Sustainable success is a muscle that takes time and commitment to grow. The mind and nervous system need conditioning to attune themselves to a new reality. In this sense, the delay between planting the seed and eating the fruit is a necessary gift. The universe is always on time.

Monetization for creatives.

Aspiring creatives might feel stuck in a career that doesn't align with their purpose. (I understand; I've been there.) To them I would say this: *cheat on your day job*. You don't have to quit your job and take a huge financial risk. Rather, use this time to start building your skills and expertise in your desired area. I wrote my entire first book while working full time in advertising, using the time before and after work to write and pitch to publishers.

Making money as an artist doesn't happen overnight. Like success in all fields, it requires determination, commitment, and the willingness to get back up after you fall down. But luckily there are plenty of opportunities. If you're having a hard time knowing where to start, the following list provides an overview of ways to generate income with creativity.

1. Sell products

The most direct way an artist can make money is to sell their work. Products can take a number of forms: paintings, books, clothing, posters, merch, ceramics, jewelry, or NFTs (non-fungible tokens). Websites like Etsy and social media platforms like Instagram make selling products easier than ever. The cost of production and distribution need to be taken into consideration. Usually, a large volume of products needs to be sold for a business to be profitable. Selling products is a good source of supplemental income for artists starting to make a name for themselves.

2. Sell experiences

Some creatives have a talent for hosting events, doing live performances, and bringing people together. This can be done both online or in person. It could be a musical performance, an interactive workshop, a festival, or some sort of immersive experience. Events and performances can be a lot of work to put together, but unlike selling products, you can sell numerous tickets to the same event, therefore maximizing profitability.

3. Work with clients

Rather than selling directly to consumers, another option is being paid by clients to do work on their behalf, such as design, writing, social media, website development, and marketing. You can work with clients on a freelance basis or as part of a company, such as an advertising agency. Working with clients is a great way to turn creativity into steady income. Of course, client work doesn't usually provide the same freedom of expression as personal art, but creativity within the boundaries of a specific objective can still be rewarding and fun.

4. Monetize an audience

The internet provides all sorts of ways for creatives to grow an audience, including social media, podcasts, and YouTube, but a following doesn't necessarily translate to making money. Having a captive audience that cares about what you share is valuable, both to you and to advertisers. The bigger the audience, the more interest you will receive. Promoting other brands is a nice way for creatives to earn income. Just be sure to work only with brands you actually like and support. You don't want to dilute the authenticity of your message.

5. Teach or coach

If you have a talent in a certain creative area, chances are someone else is willing to pay you to teach them your skills. You could offer private lessons, teach a class or workshop, or sell coaching and consultation services. For example, after I became well known as a meme artist, I created an online class called Meme School where I taught the art and science of memes. Also, based on my experience in brand strategy, I offer coaching and consultation services to help individuals develop their personal brands and launch creative projects.

6. Apply creativity to business

Being an entrepreneur is inherently creative. Launching a business requires just as much creative thinking as making art, if not more. Think about the type of business you'd like to launch. What sort of product or service does the world need? You can also apply a creative mindset to your current job. Working from a place of intuition and imagination—always looking for new solutions to old problems—will help you advance in your career faster than merely following orders.

Creativity is in high demand.

For too long, our educational and economic systems have trained people to behave like factory workers: be obedient, follow orders, optimize productivity, and don't ask too many questions. But this approach is less relevant in our rapidly changing, uncertain world. Technology and automation have replaced old jobs and created new ones. Gone are the days when someone graduated from a university, got a job in their chosen practice, and proceeded to keep the same job for forty years. The economy today is fluid, unpredictable, and ever changing. Not only will you change jobs, you will likely change careers, perhaps multiple times. Creativity is more important than ever—not just for artists but for everyone.

Albert Einstein said that we cannot solve problems with the same thinking that created them. Building a better, more sustainable world requires us to build better, more sustainable systems and businesses, which requires ingenuity and creativity. The inner artist is being called to action. Only new thinking can solve old problems.

Create a marketing funnel

Creating a marketing funnel is how you turn your audience from casual acquaintances to close friends.

The top of the marketing funnel is when people first stumble across your work. This is usually with free, easily accessible content, such as social posts or YouTube videos. It's a good idea to create consistent, high-value content and put it out for free. This will help you be seen and build a reputation.

Once people have discovered you, the next layer of the funnel is interest and engagement. You need to make an action available for your audience to go deeper. This could mean subscribing to your podcast or email newsletter, joining a free online community, or buying your book—any low-stakes action that deepens the relationship.

This is all meant to funnel people to the point of conversion and loyalty. Once someone has been in your orbit, engaged with your work, and established trust in you, they are ready for a stronger commitment. This could mean buying your paintings, attending your concerts, taking your classes, or hiring you as a coach or consultant. Don't force it. Gently flirt with your audience until they're ready for a date, then finally for a committed relationship.

WHAT

MAKES YOU

DIFFERENT

IS YOUR

SUPERPOWER

DON'T TAKE REJECTION PERSONALLY

CREATIVES SHOULD BE LIKE GOLDFISH:

 HAVE A VERY SHORT MEMORY.

IF IT DOESN'T OPEN, IT'S NOT YOUR DOOR.

LET IT GO. KEEP MOVING.

IT'S NOT REJECTION. IT'S REDIRECTION.

Chapter 14

THE NEW RENAISSANCE: CREATIVITY AND SOCIAL IMPACT

"I speak a new language,

as is always the first sign

of a new age."

SAUL WILLIAMS

BEING A DREAMER, it is sometimes said, is a waste of time and doesn't make a productive contribution to society. But dreams always come before reality. Before something can exist, it must be built. Before it can be built, it must be planned. And before it can be planned, it must be imagined. Artists are the visionaries who plant seeds in the collective consciousness that take root and eventually grow into the sturdy branches of reality. Being attuned to the quiet wisdom of intuition, artists are the first to hear the call of change, of revolution, and then reflect back the message through creative expression.

When it comes to shaping a better world, everyone has a different role, a different purpose. Some people are here to challenge the status quo and tear down old structures. Some people are here to help heal trauma. Some people are here to build more sustainable supply chains. Some people are here to make music that guides us to a higher vibration. Some people are here to transmute pain into laughter. Creativity has an essential social utility. Art is not a plan. Art is a vision. Visions always precede plans. Imagination precedes discovery.

Art changes culture.

Art is upstream of culture. Where the spirit of creativity flows, society follows. Art exists beyond borders and social constructs. It transcends race, religion, and nationality. It opens our minds to new perspectives and helps us see our shared humanity.

Since its inception, the United States of America has been an experiment in cultural integration. European settlers came from a variety of ethnic and cultural backgrounds: Irish Catholics, English Protestants, Quakers, Scandinavian farmers, Russian Jews, Dutch peasants, and more. They came seeking both freedom from religious persecution and new economic opportunities. But not all of America's cultural integration was benign or well intentioned. The nation was founded upon the colonization of Indigenous tribes who had tended the land for centuries. And the importation and enslavement of African people is a deep wound in our cultural fabric that has yet to be fully healed. What was the American dream for some has been a nightmare for others.

For better and worse, we have been thrown together, a racial and cultural melting pot, left to sort out our differences and weave a new cultural fabric from our diverse threads. Art, I believe, is the most effective loom—the instrument that blends our unique perspectives into a shared, beautiful tapestry.

When Europeans arrived in North America, they brought with them the songs, melodies, dances, instruments, and stories from their homelands, including Celtic folk ballads, English nursery rhymes, and orally recited poetry and fables handed down for generations. Poor, working-class people (especially in the southern regions near the Appalachian Mountains) entertained themselves by playing the fiddle and harmonica, singing whatever songs they could remember, and dancing around fires. Gradually, a shared musical language began to develop from these disparate traditions.

Meanwhile, other musical styles started to bubble up in the muddy waters of Mississippi and the swampy bayous of Louisiana. When Africans were taken from their homeland, they were stripped of their songs, their religions, their languages, and even their names, and they were forced to adopt the customs of their captors. But even in captivity, the human spirit finds a way to shine through. In secret, the earliest African Americans practiced the spiritual rituals of their homeland, doing their best to stay connected to their cultural heritage and keep their religious and creative traditions alive. The much-maligned Voodoo religion was developed as a vehicle to practice African rituals under the guise of Catholicism.

In New Orleans, slaves congregated in Congo Square after dark to dance and sing together, first in their native African tongues and later in English. They gradually began adopting instruments like the fiddle and trumpet. Little by little, a new culture began to emerge—a culture rooted in the African spirit and filtered through the language and aesthetics of North America.

By the 1860s (the same decade Abraham Lincoln signed the Emancipation Proclamation, which finally freed the slaves) Black people in the southern part of the United States had mastered the guitar and developed a soulful style of music that we now call the blues, which transmuted their pain and struggle into beautiful art.

This music remained largely unknown in the national consciousness until the early twentieth century, when ambitious blues singers began leaving the southern backwoods and traveling along Highway 61—the central nervous system of American music—to bring their soulful singing and guitar licks to cities like New Orleans, Memphis, St. Louis, and Chicago, creating a uniquely African imprint on American culture.

By the 1920s, the recording industry was promoting two primary categories of music. The first was called "hillbilly" music, the sound that emerged from the Appalachian Mountains and descended from European folk music. This would later be renamed "country and western." The second category was called "race records," the sound that had emerged from the Deep South with roots tracing back to African music. This would later be categorized as "rhythm and blues." Each style encompassed numerous influences from the past, but a racial divide still persisted between the music that could be traced back to Europe and Africa respectively.

Whereas a king or president can issue a decree to change the laws of the land, only art has the power to penetrate the soul and change the hearts and minds of the people. Before the United States was racially integrated from a legal perspective, it was integrated from a musical perspective. The initial catalyst was rock 'n' roll, a genre that combined elements of country and western with rhythm and blues, bringing the two winding roads of American music together in one technicolor splash.

Rock 'n' roll changed the world. The drumbeat was primal. The lyrics were raw. Singers danced and shook their hips. The audience screamed. It was a cathartic release, a physical salvation in the tradition of old African-American spirituals. Rock 'n' roll was undeniable because it spoke directly to the body. Like a sexual impulse, it transcended the socially constructed objections of the mind.

The rock 'n' roll revolution of the early 1950s was the first time that the majority of White and Black audiences were listening to the same music. Art cut through the cultural divide. And although Elvis Presley would be the artist to emerge with the most notoriety, Elvis could not have been Elvis without the influence of Black artists who came before him, like B. B. King, Little Richard, and Fats Domino.

Elvis Presley grew up in the Deep South, in a poor Mississippi neighborhood. He attended Black churches and learned their songs, absorbing the spirit of blues and gospel, that same spirit which had descended from Voodoo, from slave songs, from tribal African celebrations. It was the acceptance and integration of this spirit that made rock 'n' roll music one of the greatest art forms of the twentieth century.

America would not be America without the New Orleans slave songs, the trumpet of Louis Armstrong, the piano of Thelonious Monk, the voice of Billie Holiday, the guitar of Jimi Hendrix, the wisdom of Maya Angelou, the inner vision of Stevie Wonder, the dance moves of James Brown, the confidence of Muhammad Ali, the brushstrokes of Jean-Michel Basquiat, and the soulful lyrics of Tupac Shakur.

Dogma must be challenged and dissolved in the imagination and the heart before it can be overcome in the material world. Art points the way to a society beyond borders, beyond hate, beyond division.

A civilization in crisis.

As I write these words in the early years of the 2020s, our civilization is facing a multifaceted crisis: economic, environmental, political, existential, spiritual. Our legacy systems—propped up by colonialism, greed, and economic imbalance—exist in a prolonged state of atrophy, disconnected from the regenerative flow of nature. The problems are deeply rooted and systemic. It often feels hopeless. What can we as individuals do to help heal the world?

There are historical precedents. In the fourteenth century, a period known as the Dark Ages, Europe was haunted by religious persecution, famine, and plagues. The future looked bleak, but the artists, the philosophers, and the dreamers found a way forward. Taking inspiration from ancient Greece, artists like Leonardo da Vinci, Michelangelo, and Raphael studied the timeless beauty of classical art and philosophy, and they adapted the style for their times. Creative innovation was not relegated to the visual arts. Leonardo da Vinci's innovation extended into science and engineering, taking inspiration from nature and adding human ingenuity to imagine and design practical tools for the future. This small group of creatives, who were willing to think and act outside the box, led to a flourishing culture, starting in Italy before spreading across Europe, shedding the light of modernity into the Dark Ages. This period came to be known as the Renaissance, the French word for "rebirth."

Art is not just art. It can be a seed of new consciousness, a vision, a prophecy. The languages of art, stories, and myth are just as important and true as the language of science. Art can articulate a collective feeling and ignite a change of mind and heart. Art is a dream that solidifies into higher and higher fidelity according to our collective awareness and belief, eventually becoming real.

> "Artists to my mind are the real architects of change,
>
> and not the political legislators who
>
> implement change after the fact."
>
> WILLIAM S. BURROUGHS

Even the Greek philosopher Plato, an early proponent of logic and reason, believed that art could have ripple effects that altered the fabric of society. In his book *The Republic*, considered the crown jewel of Western philosophy, Plato stated that music had the authority to change laws. "Musical innovation is full of danger to the State," he said. "For when modes of music change, the fundamental laws of the State always change with them."

This is a call to artists everywhere. What we need is a New Renaissance, a new vision to believe in, a vision rooted in sustainability, community, and higher consciousness. We need a new cultural myth.

Planting new myths.

Myths are the deeply rooted stories upon which the laws, culture, and values of a society are based; they are the shared moral bedrock of a civilization. Myths come in all shapes and sizes, from religious gods to creation stories to mythical creatures to fables and parables to popular children's movies like *The Little Mermaid* or the *Harry Potter* series, which have inspired generations. Myths are not literally true; they are figuratively true. They represent archetypal dramas that teach us the essence of truth. Myths are the deepest agreements at the heart of a culture, the invisible fabric that binds us together.

Myths are proto-memes, ideas and stories that go viral and take root within a civilization. From the roots of mythology grow the branches of religion, philosophy, and politics. When the roots are strong, the branches are healthy, but when the roots of mythology are disrupted or forgotten, the branches of society will atrophy and eventually die.

The dominant myths of Western civilization are derived from Christianity and the principles of reason and logic brought on by the eighteenth-century Age of Enlightenment. Whether or not you believe Christianity is literally true hardly matters. Our society has been built upon its moral foundation. For millennia, Christianity has informed our legal system, our foreign policy, our schools, and our unspoken social dynamics—for better and worse. (For example, the Ten Commandments from the Old Testament are still displayed in many United States courthouses.) This connective tissue has given us a shared understanding of morality, whether or not we subscribe to the faith-based aspects of the religion.

The irony is that the Christian story was subverted and misinterpreted by the same power structures that its original myth-weavers stood in opposition to, and the message of universal love was distorted to justify "holy wars" and dogmatic oppression.

In recent centuries, the shared myths holding our culture together have started to unravel, causing our social structures to become unstable. This is what Friedrich Nietzsche meant when he famously proclaimed "God is dead" in the 1880s. He wasn't implying that some literal God had actually died, but rather that our collective attention had turned in another direction. Instead of being unified under a shared vision, we have been broken into fragments, isolated by subjective reality tunnels.

Some people blame the internet and social media, where curated feeds serve as echo chambers that accelerate fragmentation through confirmation bias. Others blame an increase in moral degradation. If we throw away the belief in God, it's only a matter of time until the values inspired by God also crumble. Even art has played a role in the demoralization of society. The modus operandi of twentieth-century art was not unification but deconstruction. The creative thrust of the period was further and further abstraction and the systematic dismantling of the idols and ideals of Christianity, of the Renaissance, of the Enlightenment.

Cubism, one of several art movements led by the master of abstraction, Pablo Picasso, was art's way of saying that there is no single objective reality. Instead, there are endless perspectives overlapping in a tapestry of subjectivity. Surrealism melted reality into a strange and symbolic Freudian dream. Pointillism reduced the world to tiny dots, mirroring the scientific discovery of subatomic particles. And finally, with abstract impressionism, content was removed altogether, replaced with bold and aimless brushstrokes, almost like someone was painting over—and thereby erasing—all of art history, leaving only a blank slate, a chance to start over.

The philosophy informing much of twentieth- and twenty-first-century art, culture, and academia is postmodernism, a school of thought characterized by a distrust of grand narratives and ideologies. According to postmodernism, truth is relative. All so-called realities are merely mental constructs reinforced by social expectations. Those in power set the terms of the game for everyone else. The proper role of art, therefore, is to challenge and deconstruct our arbitrary ideas of meaning and certainty, and to equalize the playing field in terms of personal identity and perspective.

This philosophy certainly has merit. After all, the world, including our myths and religions, is far from perfect. We do not, and never have, lived in Utopia. As much as Western civilization has been a wellspring of prosperity to some, it has also been a dominating colonizer to others. When the values of society are not living up to their highest potential, we are right to challenge them.

> "We cannot evolve faster than our language. If we appear to be confronted by unsolvable problems, it's because we have the wrong language for dealing with these problems. You learn that with computers. Certain languages are good for certain kinds of problems. We have to constantly evolve language and push it forward."
>
> TERENCE MCKENNA

The problem with postmodernism is that it does not offer a viable alternative of meaning. The vision is empty. Deconstruction alone does not a culture make. As such, we have lost our connection to the subtle language of myth. The public discourse has devolved into argumentative absolutes, everyone convinced of the righteousness of their own opinion.

We are lost in the details, unable to see the big picture that connects us, united only by our shared outrage and confusion. The question is: *How can we challenge and revolutionize our social systems without deconstructing ourselves into oblivion?*

Terence McKenna addressed this issue in a lecture called "Opening the Doors of Creativity," delivered in 1990.

> "In a way, it's the poets who have failed us," he said, "because they have not provided a song or sung a vision that we could all move in concert to. So now we are in the absurd position of being able to do anything, and what we are doing is fouling our own nest and pushing ourselves toward planetary toxification and extinction. This is because the poets, the artists, have not articulated a moral vision. The moral vision must come from the unconscious. It doesn't have to do, I believe, with these post-meaning movements in art: deconstructionism and this sort of thing . . . Art's task is to save the soul of mankind . . . Anything less is a dithering while Rome burns. Because if the artists cannot find the way, then the way cannot be found."

If the sustained dream of artists and poets helps to shape a culture's mythology, and that mythology goes on to generate values, laws, and morality, then the artists and poets of the twenty-first century have a responsibility to renew our shared mythology and vision. We must go back to the soil and plant new seeds in the collective consciousness. Artists are the magicians and the mythmakers. We need new language—better language—to elevate the tone of the conversation. A new Earth must be born in the heart and the imagination before it can manifest as physical reality.

The New Renaissance.

Time is cyclical. More accurately, time is a spiral. We circle back to the past while also progressing upward. As Mark Twain suggested, history doesn't repeat exactly, but it always rhymes. Our contemporary lack of meaningful myths presents an opportunity to renew the lessons of old, forgotten myths, such as Indigenous stories that acknowledge our connection to nature and the supreme importance of the Goddess.

In the Dark Ages, when humanity had seemingly reached a dead end, the artists and philosophers reached back to ancient Greece to find a semblance of order to build upon. The redemption of classical idealism gave birth to the Renaissance. According to Terence McKenna, our problems today are so severe that, to find our way out of the mess, we must look even farther back into history to reclaim the natural order that we have lost. McKenna referred to this collective remembering as the Archaic Revival.

"We must now reach back into time for a new cultural model," McKenna said. "Our crisis is so great that we have to reach back to the high Paleolithic to the moment immediately before the invention of agriculture and the creation of the dominator ego."

This "dominator ego" has been the driving force of civilization for thousands of years. It's not a specific person, a group of people, or even a conscious ideology. It's a mind virus. Under the mantra "me over we," this virus has conquered, colonized, raped, and pillaged the world, disconnecting us from ourselves and each other.

The problem of the dominator-ego mind virus is one our creativity must address. It's not a problem for creativity alone; but artists, as our mythmakers and image setters, can help point the way forward and inspire a change of heart and mind. This means redirecting the story of art away from the genius of personal achievement and toward community and service. It means being conscious of how our words and actions, like memes, create ripples that impact the world. It means balancing logic with intuition and placing the wisdom of yin on an equal level with the action-oriented yang perspective.

Decolonizing art and language.

In his book *The Alphabet versus the Goddess*, Leonard Shlain argues that although the development of language has been an amazing tool for humanity in many ways, it has also distorted our experience of reality into an overly linear and logical framework, depriving us of a wider and more holistic perspective that came naturally to our preliterate ancestors. There is a conflict, this theory suggests, between written language—which hyperfocuses our attention on mental abstractions—and the natural world, which is infinitely small and vast and ever changing. Words are merely symbols, and a symbol is not the thing itself, and much nuance is lost in the translation from experience to semantics.

With humanity's reliance on written language came a dominance of the left hemisphere of the brain, which emphasizes logic and rationality over emotion and empathy. This shift—subtle and gradual—eventually led to a dominating colonial mentality and the suppression of both women and yin wisdom. Our language and literature flourished, along with our ability to manipulate and control.

Language is a powerful and neutral tool. Like fire, it can be used both to help and to harm. Decolonizing language means loosening the tight grip of literal, logical certainty to make room for the softer language of myth and metaphor. More than one perspective can be true at once. We must be willing to expand the lens of our perception to see, feel, and understand subtle information beyond the reach of rigid logic.

Growing up in rural Minnesota, I lived near a Dakota Sioux community. During a few summer evenings, I was invited to attend their powwow ceremonies, where they danced, sang, and told stories. On one such occasion, a Dakota elder shared a prophecy about the eagle and the condor. According to this legend, thousands of years ago humanity was split into two paths. The path of the eagle was defined by mind, science, and technology. The path of the condor was defined by heart, intuition, and spirit. The condor people (located primarily in the Southern Hemisphere) cultivated the same ancient traditions, while the eagle people (located primarily in the Northern Hemisphere) sought technological progress and the self-actualization of the individual.

For many centuries, these two paths have been disconnected — the right and left hands of humanity out of sync. But according to the prophecy, the eagle and the condor will one day reunite to share and integrate each other's wisdom, restoring balance to the earth.

The prophecy of the eagle and the condor helps articulate the role of art in shaping a better world. Following are six principles to inspire the New Renaissance in art and culture.

Principles of the New Renaissance.

1. Connection to nature

Art is not a mental abstraction. It grows from humanity just as we grow from nature. Learning from the patterns and cycles of the natural world and integrating these lessons into our art is a way to align our individual creativity with the nature of creation.

2. Interdependence

No person is an island. We depend on each other. The antidote to ego (me first) is community (we first). Acknowledging the interdependence of all life as a shared ecosystem is essential for our future. Art that is community driven, both in its creation and consumption, can help bring the tribe of humanity closer together.

3. The Goddess

For every god, there is a goddess. The worship of the Goddess has been suppressed by the dominator-ego mind virus for centuries. It's time to restore her rightful seat on the throne. This doesn't mean replacing a patriarchy with an equally imbalanced matriarchy. It means restoring harmony by cultivating intuition and yin energy across all facets of society.

4. Social utility

As we reshape society based on the principles of sustainability and community, there will be an increased role for creativity, art, and design in helping the world *work better*. Joining forces with architecture, engineering, city planning, and technology, artists can imagine new ways in which their art can be applied, not merely consumed. This harkens back to the Renaissance vision of Leonardo da Vinci, who merged art and engineering to conjure technological solutions that were aligned with the laws of nature.

5. Techno-dharma

"Techno-dharma" is a term I learned from my friend Michael Phillip, host of the podcast *Third Eye Drops*. It implies a convergence of wisdom and technology. The digital landscape is accelerating at a rapid pace and is unlikely to slow down anytime soon. What does art look like in the age of virtual reality and artificial intelligence? Instead of being used by technology, how can we leverage technology as a tool and creative medium for good?

6. Consciousness

What is the origin of sentience? The prevailing scientific theory is that consciousness is a random result of increasingly complex matter. In other words, matter creates mind. But innovators in the fields of neuroscience and psychology are beginning to question this narrative and suggest that consciousness could be a more fundamental reality than space and time. This so-called new science harkens back to the ancient wisdom of Buddhism, the Vedic tradition, and shamanism. Perhaps, to a degree, matter is residual of consciousness, not the other way around. At the very least, the relationship between matter and consciousness deserves further, open-minded investigation.

One morning in 2021, when the world felt especially heavy and hopeless, I closed my eyes to envision what a post-dominator-ego society might look like. The following poem, which is only one sentence long, came to me like a lightning flash.

"A New Earth"

When the parasites have been removed, and the oceans have been cleaned, and the virus of fear of each other and ourselves has been blessed and transmuted by the great Amazonian grandmothers, and we have shed the dead skin of history, and the hyperrational, disembodied laws have been replaced by the organic, regenerative decrees of nature, and we've finally embraced our own magic and divinity and made peace with Father Death, and there's not an ounce of judgment left because we understand that judgment of another is judgment of the self, and every McDonald's has been turned into a garden, and every shopping mall converted into a place of worship, and we celebrate each Spring Equinox by electing a single yellow daisy as president of the world in a symbolic gesture of gentleness and the futility of control, then we shall wake up in the dewy grass of the new dawn and see our own reflections in the faces of each other and in the sunlight above.

We speak reality into existence.

There is a reason we "spell" words. Words literally cast a spell. The old magician word *abracadabra* actually derives from a Hebrew phrase meaning "I will create as I speak." All matter, at its essence, is energy vibrating at different frequencies. The universe is a symphony of sound. Words are vibrations (spells) that cocreate the music—and magic—of reality.

We are both empowered and restricted by our use of language. The words of a president can be used to declare war. The words of a revolutionary can be used to declare independence. Your words can make someone fall in love with you, or hire you, or fire you. They can be used to spark laughter and heartbreak. The language in a legal contract is designed to narrow and restrict, to box people into the terms of the agreement. The language of the poet is designed to unlock the mind and set consciousness free.

Language is the source code of the matrix, our primary interface with the operating system of reality. It seems to me that we, as Western civilization, have fallen into a trap of rigid thinking and argumentative absolutes because we have forgotten the subtle languages of poetry and myth.

Every day, with our thoughts, our words, and our art, we are perpetuating one meme or another. Ideas are the virus, and we are the carriers. What virus, what meme, are you spreading? Being an artist is about consciously choosing the ideas and myths we carry and pass on to others. This is what conscious communication and creativity are all about: to inspire change with our words and art.

Instead of giving your valuable energy and awareness to rigid and disempowering narratives, use the seeds of your imagination, words, and art to plant a new reality. Become the magician and mythmaker. Start casting better spells.

Plant a new vision

Art, music, language, and other creative fields have a profound impact on society. You can argue a point of view until you're blue in the face, but this won't have the same resonance as a work of art that cuts through the intellectual clutter to make a direct impact on the heart.

For this exercise, we are going to articulate a vision for a better world, a New Renaissance. Perhaps your vision isn't "new" at all, but rather a return to the wisdom of the ancient past. Using the creative medium of your choice (it could be a drawing, a poem, a song, a collage, a social media post), express a vision for the world you wish to see. Don't focus on the problems of today. Root your art in a world where those problems are already solved. How have they been solved? It doesn't matter. Just like every creative project, it helps to visualize the end from the beginning. We are not trying to build—not yet. We are trying to dream, to plant a seed in the imagination, inspiring a vision that we can work toward.

A few things to consider:

- What is the seed you wish to plant in the collective consciousness?

- What does the world look like when natural balance has been restored?

- What aspects of our social systems (political, legal, etc.) would you like to change?

- How is society different when the yin is no longer suppressed?

- What is a story or myth that can help to heal the future?

After your art is finished, share it with as many people as possible. Have a discussion around it. You can even start a group and invite your friends to plant a vision of their own. Get the vision out of your head and into the world. Be the meme that you want to go viral.

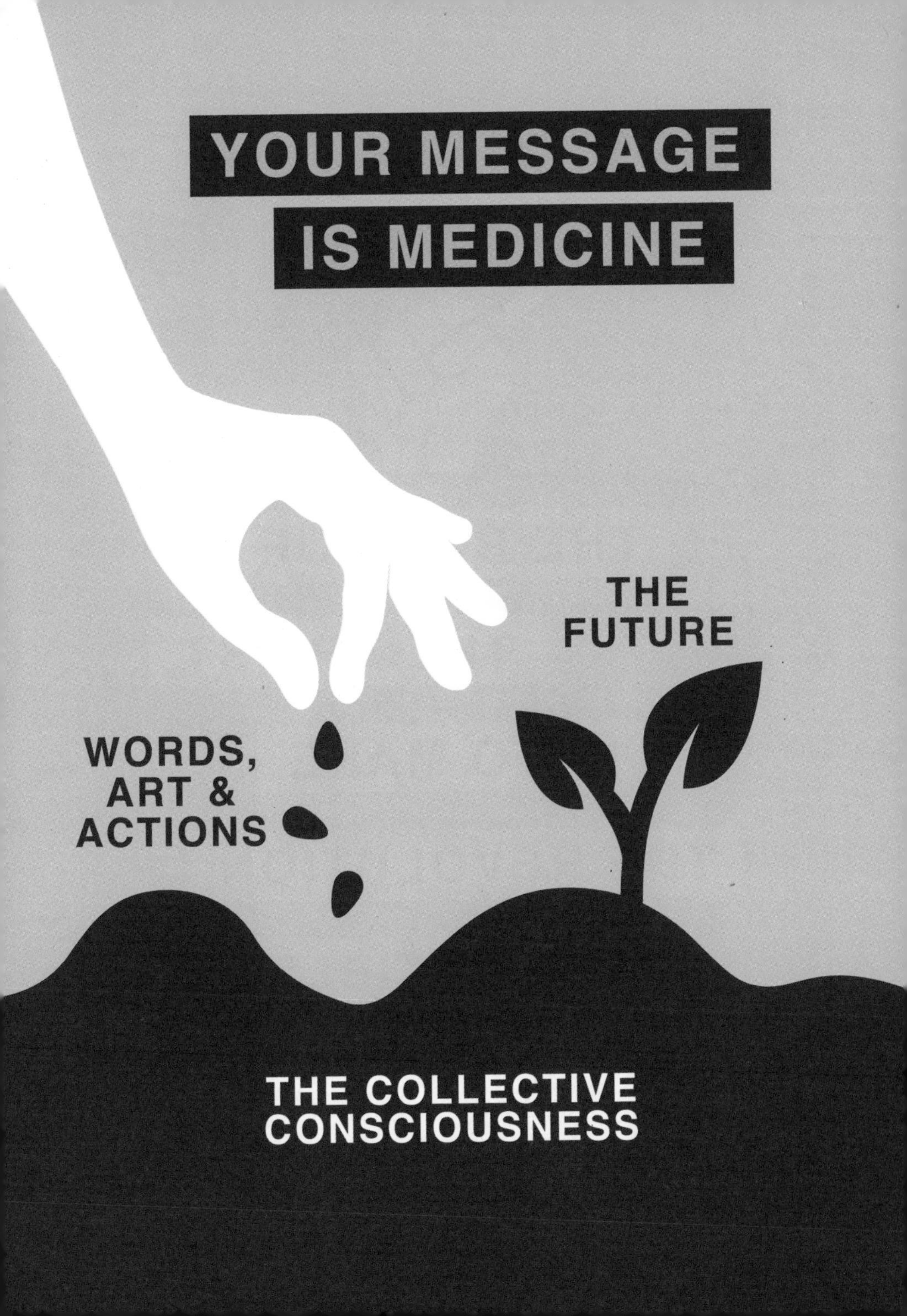
YOUR MESSAGE
IS MEDICINE
THE
FUTURE
WORDS,
ART &
ACTIONS
THE COLLECTIVE
CONSCIOUSNESS

THE ROLE OF
THE ARTIST
IS TO MAKE
THE REVOLUTION
IRRESISTIBLE

– TONI CADE BAMBARA

OLD STORY	NEW STORY
WE CLAIM WHAT WE WANT WITH FORCE	WE RECLAIM THE WISDOM WE HAVE FORGOTTEN
WE MUST CONSTANTLY HUSTLE TO GENERATE WEALTH	SUSTAINABLE SYSTEMS REGENERATE VALUE
WE STRIVE TO FIT INTO THE BOX OF SOCIAL EXPECTATIONS	OUR ACTIONS ARE ALIGNED WITH PURPOSE
NATURE IS A COMMODITY TO PLUNDER & EXPLOIT	NATURE IS A PRICELESS ECOSYSTEM THAT SUSTAINS US
ART IS AN EXPRESSION OF PERSONAL GENIUS	ART IS A GIFT & SERVICE TO THE COMMUNITY

YOUR CREATIVE SIGNATURE

WHAT'S YOUR CREATIVE SIGNATURE?

"This above all:
to thine own self be true."

WILLIAM SHAKESPEARE

NO TWO CREATIVES are alike. Your artistic fingerprint is a unique culmination of your personality, taste, beliefs, and life experiences. Nobody can replicate who you are as a person and an artist. Your unique combination of gifts and vision is yours alone.

Being creative is not about copying anyone else. It's about excavating what is already inside you, like a sculptor chipping away at stone until only the statue remains. The better you know yourself, the more clarity you will have as an artist.

The following section is a workshop to help you determine Your Creative Signature. It's designed to make you dig deep below the surface to discover what's ticking inside. Don't worry, there are no wrong answers. The point is to be honest and see what answers arise naturally. You can either complete the workshop all at once or dedicate a day to each section. Don't rush. Take your time to meditate and reflect on one question at a time.

Have fun!

Purpose

Every artist has a different motivation and intention. Your purpose is your North Star, the underlying reason why you create. When we work without a purpose, the result is shallow and uninspired. Knowing your purpose gives you direction.

- What is your reason or motivation to be creative? What do you hope to achieve? For example:

    to make money

    to get unstuck

    to heal my inner child

    to grow an audience

    to change the world

    to have fun

    other

- What are some of your natural strengths or talents?

- Does your art have any underlying political, social, or spiritual messages? If so, what are they?

- What kind of impact do you want your art to make in the world? Think big.

- Which part of the creative process do you find most exciting?

Audience

Art doesn't exist in a vacuum. It's a relationship between the creator and the consumer. Who is your audience? It's probably not "everyone."

Different art appeals to different people. Understanding your audience doesn't mean you should conform your art to fit their expectations. Sometimes we need to challenge and surprise our audience. But knowing who your work appeals to will help to steer your purpose.

- Describe your audience. Who do you make art for? What are they like? What are their attitudes and behaviors? Be as specific as possible.

- What does your audience enjoy most about your work? In other words, what makes your art lovable?

- What emotions do you want to elicit in your audience?

- Imagine that your creativity is medicine. What problem or ailment are you helping to heal in your audience?

- How does your audience typically discover your work?

- Are there any other unexplored ways that your audience could find you? List as many as you can think of.

Territory

Your territory is where your art is positioned and situated within your industry and in the world. This includes your genre, key themes, and differentiation from similar artists. If all the art in the world was a giant map, your territory is where you reside.

- What, exactly, do you make? What form does your work take?

- What are the recurring themes in your work? (They could be either abstract or specific.)

- If your art is a movie, what genre is it and why?

- What does your work depict? In other words, what is the primary subject matter?

- Who are some of the current artists in your field who you admire?

- What differentiates your work from other artists in your field?

Style

Your style includes all aesthetic elements of your work: the flavors, textures, colors, attitudes, and personality. Style is a sandbox where you can play and experiment with technique. There is no right or wrong style. It's a matter of subjective taste. It's okay to have a very defined style. It's also okay to mix it up and try different things. Some artists completely reinvent themselves every few years.

- What are three words that describe your aesthetic style?

- If someone saw your work without your name attached, what are distinguishing features that could be identified as yours?

- What would your art be if it were:

    a location

    a meal

    an outfit

    a season

    a feeling

    a song

    an animal

a historical figure

a color

- Choose the word in each pair that best describes your art:

  Classic   or   Innovative

  Energetic or   Calm

  Mystical   or   Scientific

  Complex   or   Minimal

  Serious   or   Playful

  Edgy   or   Sweet

Influences

What we consume impacts what we create. Our art is the culmination of our influences. Every artist is a lineage holder of certain traditions, ideas, or styles. We take the baton from those who came before and pass it along to the next generation. Knowing your influences is about understanding your artistic lineage and carrying the torch with respect and intention.

- When did you first discover your chosen art form? Who were the first creators who made you excited about art?

- Which creators had the biggest influence on your overall philosophy and outlook?

- Which creators had the biggest influence on your style and aesthetic?

- Did anyone in your personal life have a big impact on your art? Who was it?

- Do you consider yourself to be part of any artist lineage or movement? If so, what is it?

- Imagine that you are being inducted into the Creative Hall of Fame after a hugely successful career. You can choose one artist from any point in history to give an introduction speech. Who do you choose and why?

Vision

Your vision is the long-term goal and intention you hold for yourself. It's best not to be too fixed or rigid. We want to hold space for opportunities that we can't yet see. But having a clear idea in your mind about what you want to make and who you want to become (even if that idea changes over time) will help draw you toward your intended reality.

- Describe your ideal creative project if time and money were not factors.

- What are some ways you would like to work with others? Describe your ideal creative partnership or collaboration.

- Imagine that, one year from today, you are featured on the front page of the *New York Times*. Best-case scenario, what does the headline say?

- Imagine yourself in five years if there were no obstacles. What kind of art are you making? Where are you living? How are you spending your time?

Your Creative Signature

Now that you have reflected on each question, let's distill each category down to a single statement. Complete each of the following sentences.

Try to keep each answer to a single sentence. Brevity is the gateway to clarity.

My purpose is:

My audience is:

My territory is:

My style is:

My influences are:

My vision is:

WAYS TO BE AN ARTIST
(AN INCOMPLETE LIST)

BELIEVE
IN MAGIC

LIVE WITH
INTENTION

GIVE YOURSELF
PERMISSION
TO CHANGE

DANCE WITH
YOUR FEARS

~~BE PERFECT~~

CHOOSE
WONDER OVER
WORRY

EXPLORE
BEYOND YOUR
COMFORT ZONE

SAY OLD
THINGS IN
NEW WAYS

FIND BEAUTY
IN THE
MUNDANE

~~HAVE IT ALL
FIGURED OUT~~

EMBRACE
YOUR QUIRKS

ORGANIZE
YOUR ROOM

SPEND TIME
IN NATURE

DO SOMETHING
UNEXPECTED

BE CURIOUS

DISSOLVE
BOUNDARIES

THINK LIKE
A CHILD

~~ALWAYS BE
INSPIRED~~

~~COMPARE
YOURSELF
TO OTHERS~~

TRANSMUTE
PAIN INTO
ART

SEEK NOVEL
EXPERIENCES

TREAT IT
LIKE A GAME

STUDY OTHER
ARTISTS

IMAGINE
A BETTER
WORLD

THE
ARTIST'S PLEDGE

**I PROMISE TO KEEP
CREATING, TO REMAIN
CURIOUS, TO TRUST MY
INSTINCTS, TO IMAGINE
A BETTER WORLD, TO
APPRECIATE BEAUTY, TO
TAKE RISKS, TO FEEL MY
FEAR AND DO IT ANYWAY,
TO KEEP SHOWING UP NO
MATTER HOW HOPELESS
IT SEEMS, TO GIVE MY
MIND AND FEET SPACE
TO WANDER, TO KEEP
EXPLORING THE DARKNESS
IN SEARCH OF LIGHT**

Afterword

CREATIVITY IS YOUR NATURE

"It is our mission on Earth to combat false teachings
by manifesting the truth which is in us. Even
singlehanded we can accomplish miracles."

HENRY MILLER

WHAT IS THE purpose of being human? The most fundamental purpose is to create. What you create doesn't matter. The act of creation is an everyday activity. Just as a frog is born to jump and a bird is born to fly, we are born to make our thought forms manifest on the physical plane. This is our nature, our dharma. The life force that animates the human body is a living expression of source creation.

Each cell in our bodies exists in a perpetual state of regeneration. The mind is a sophisticated antenna that picks up signals from unknown realms through the portal of imagination and intuition. The hands and fingers are intricate tools designed to write and build new worlds into existence. The tongue is a magic wand that bends vocal cord sounds into syllables that cast spells into the collective imagination through the alchemy of language.

Every day we use our thoughts, words, intentions, and actions to shape our personal realities, like baby gods practicing the game of creation. The next time you're feeling stuck, remember the miracle and mystery of your existence. You don't need to strive for creativity as something outside yourself. Sink into your nature. Move on instinct. Let your life force express itself without hesitation. You're already an artist.

Creativity benefits us in several ways. It is emotionally cathartic, intellectually stimulating, and spiritually uplifting. It helps us process our thoughts and feelings. It is a healing modality that reconnects us with our inner child, a part of us that may be traumatized, suppressed, or forgotten. With creativity comes curiosity, playfulness, and a sense of wonder, which allow us to move from a state of fear to faith, from doubt to trust, from discord to harmony.

It doesn't matter if your work remains unseen or if you become a famous artist. Each time you lift a paintbrush, open your mouth to speak in public, launch a new business, or drag your pen across a page, you are taking a leap into the unknown and learning to trust yourself a little bit more. Art is a ritual to exorcise the demons of trauma and awaken the inner child. It's not about being good at creativity. It's about creativity being good for you.

Change begins within ourselves. Every word, action, and piece of art we express is like casting a vote for the world we wish to see. Creativity is an agent of change. What is the change you wish to make? Point your energy and creativity in that direction. Instead of complaining about the world, demonstrate an example of a better one. Be the glitch you want to see in the matrix.

Many problems in the world stem from a collective mindset of taking. We are stuck in a pattern of extracting and hoarding resources, seeking validation for ourselves, and taking more than we give. If we are to live in a world of peace and harmony, this mentality needs to shift. We must learn to be generous, to share, to freely extend a helping hand.

What we give is not lost. It circulates and comes back, like the cycle of water that evaporates and returns as rain.

Find your magic and give it away. Your creativity is a gift to the world.

"SING ALONG"

(A POEM)

Some people die
at 25 years old
and carry on
as a well-dressed corpse
(propped up on caffeine
and pharmaceuticals)
for another 60 years.

We don't outgrow
the child inside.
We tie them up
with socially constructed rope
and toss into a closet
of embarrassment and shame
(then turn up the busyness
so we can't hear them cry).

Childhood is not
an age. It's an
attitude of curiosity
and wonder.

Each moment,
every day, we
make the choice
to celebrate
or suppress
ourselves.

And it's never
too late to change
your mind.

When was the last
time you gave yourself
permission to <u>play</u>
without agenda?

Do you dance for
no reason? Or do all
the reasons not to dance
give you heavy feet?

Those dreams
you had of flying
were not fantasy.
They were foreshadowing
the day your spirit would rise
after shedding
the dead weight
of other people's
opinions.

After all, all of this,
everything you see,
is just a sandbox,
a game of hide-and-seek
between yourself
and God.

Have you forgotten
that you were born to create?
To birth your dreams
into tangible form?
Have you forgotten
that every cell in your body
lives in a perpetual state
of regeneration?

The sacred geometry
of flesh and bone
is a living expression
of source code.
We bloom together
like momentary flowers
and return to soil
to seed new life.

Every single sunrise
sings a new verse
in the universal
sacred song.

And each breath
is your invitation
to clap your hands
and sing along.

AFFIRMATIONS
FOR ARTISTS

1. I AM NOT MY WORK.
I AM MERELY A CHANNEL.

2. THERE ARE NO MISTAKES.
MISTAKES ARE PORTALS TO
UNEXPECTED SOLUTIONS.

3. CREATIVITY IS PLAYFUL.
IF I'M NOT HAVING FUN,
I'M DOING IT WRONG.

4. I WILL LET MY WORK FLOW
THROUGH ME WITHOUT TRYING
TO MICROMANAGE THE PROCESS.

5. MY SUCCESS IS BASED ON
INNER FULFILLMENT, NOT
EXTERNAL VALIDATION.

6. I WILL NOT COMPARE MYSELF
TO OTHERS. MY ONLY COMPETITION
IS MY OWN FEAR AND SELF-DOUBT.

7. I TRUST WHERE I AM ON MY
JOURNEY. THERE IS NO HURRY.

TO CREATE, TO BRING ANY VISION TO LIFE,

IS A SPIRITUAL ACTIVITY.

GOD EXISTS WITHOUT FORM

IN THE BREATH OF THE SAXOPHONE PLAYER,

THE MOVEMENT OF THE PAINTER'S BRUSH,

THE INSTINCT OF THE FREESTYLE RAPPER,

AND THE MOTION OF A DANCING BODY.

TO BE "INSPIRED" IS TO BE "IN SPIRIT."

THERE IS NO CHURCH ON EARTH

MORE HOLY THAN THE HUMAN BODY,

A VESSEL THAT GROUNDS HEAVEN

HERE AND NOW.

BE THE MEME THAT YOU WANT TO GO VIRAL IN THE WORLD

BIBLIOGRAPHY

"I feel like I'm channeling ideas from somewhere else . . ." "Rick Rubin: Legendary Music Producer, episode 275." *Lex Friedman Podcast*. April 10, 2022. Video, 2:04:16. youtube.com/watch?v=H_szemxPcTI&list=PLrAXtmErZgOdP_8GztsuKi9nrraNbKKp4&index=92.

"To make living itself an art, that is the goal." Miller, Henry. *Big Sur and the Oranges of Hieronymus Bosch*. New York: New Directions, 1957.

"Every child is an artist . . ." Pablo Picasso, in Davidson, R. P. "Modern Living: Ozmosis in Central Park." *Time*, October 4, 1976.

"You never change things by fighting the existing reality . . ." Buckminster Fuller, in Sieden, Steven L. *A Fuller View: Buckminster Fuller's Vision of Hope and Abundance for All*. Studio City, CA: Divine Arts, 2011.

"Nature does not hurry, yet everything is accomplished." Lao Tzu. *Tao Te Ching*. Translated by Stephen Mitchell. New York: Harper Perennial Modern Classics, 2006.

"An old silent pond. A frog jumps into the pond—Splash!" Matsuo Bashō, in *Haiku Harvest*. Translated by Harry Behn. White Plains, NY: Peter Pauper Press, 1962.

"Sometimes I need only to stand wherever I am to be blessed." Oliver, Mary. *Evidence*. Boston: Beacon Press, 2010.

"I think I will do nothing for a long time but listen." Whitman, Walt. "Song of Myself" in *Leaves of Grass*. 1855.

"If your mind is empty, it is always ready . . ." Suzuki, Shunryū. *Zen Mind, Beginner's Mind*. New York: Weatherhill, 1970.

"If I have seen further than others, it is by standing . . ." Isaac Newton, 1675 letter. In Turnball, H. W., ed. *The Correspondence of Isaac Newton*. Cambridge, England: Cambridge University Press, 2008.

"The pictures were painted directly through me . . . " Hilma af Klint, from her notebooks. Bashkoff, Tracey, ed. *Hilma af Klint, Paintings for the Future*. New York: Guggenheim Museum Publications, 2018.

"I think, therefore I am." Descartes, René. *Principles of Philosophy* (1644). Translated by R. P. Miller. New York: Springer, 1982.

"Ideas are like fish. If you want to catch little fish . . ." Lynch, David. *Catching the Big Fish: Meditation, Consciousness, and Creativity*. New York: TarcherPerigee, 2007.

"The mind rebels against the unknown . . ." Krishnamurti, Jiddu. *The Book of Life: Daily Meditations with Krishnamurti*. New York: HarperOne, 1995.

"A work of art which did not begin in emotion is not art." Paul Cezanne. *Paintings, Biography, and Quotes*. paulcezanne.org/quotes.jsp.

"The spectrum of human emotion from . . ." Hawkins, David R. *Power vs. Force*. Carlsbad, CA: Hay House, 2014.

"Poetry is the one place where people can speak . . ." Ginsberg, Allen. *Spontaneous Mind: Selected Interviews 1958–1996*. Edited by

David Carter. New York: Harper Perennial, 2002.

"We live in condensations of our imagination." McKenna, Terence.
Chaos, Creativity, and Cosmic Consciousness. Rochester, VT:
Park Street Press, 2001. "Yes, I am a dreamer. For a dreamer is
one who . . ." Wilde, Oscar. "The Critic as Artist." *The Nineteenth
Century*, 1890.

"Do not fear mistakes. There are none." A discussion of this Miles Davis
quote can be found in Bertinetto, Alessandro. "'Do not fear mistakes—
there are none': The Mistake as Surprising Experience of Creativity in
Jazz." *Education as Jazz: Interdisciplinary Sketches on a New Metaphor*.
Marina Santi and Eleonora Zorzi, eds. Newcastle upon Tyne, England:
Cambridge Scholars Publishing, 2016. cambridgescholars.com
/resources/pdfs/978-1-4438-9070-0-sample.pdf.

"I saw the best minds of my generation destroyed by madness."
Ginsberg, Allen. *Howl*. San Francisco: City Lights, 1959.

"Your mind will answer most questions if you learn to relax and wait for
the answer." Burroughs, William S. *Naked Lunch*. New York: Grove
Press, 1959.

"A genius is the one most like himself." Thelonius Monk in his journals
(1960). Taylor, Tom. "Thelonious Monk's 25 Tips for Musicians."
Far Out, September 2, 2021. faroutmagazine.co.uk
/thelonious-monk-25-handwritten-tips-for-musicians.

"Style is the answer to everything . . ." Bukowski, Charles. *Love Is a
Dog from Hell*. Los Angeles: Black Sparrow Press, 1977.

"riverrun, past Eve and Adam's, from swerve . . ." Joyce, James.
Finnegans Wake. London: Faber and Faber, 1939.

"I knew who I was this morning, but I've changed . . ." Carroll, Lewis. *Alice's Adventures in Wonderland.* London: Macmillan, 1865.

"Don't think about making art, just get it done. . ." Makos, Christopher. *Warhol Memoir.* New York: Charta Books, 2004.

"Inspiration is for amateurs. . . . " Close, Chuck. *Chuck Close.* Robert Storr, Kirk Varnedoe, Deborah Wye, Glenn D. Lowry, eds. New York: The Museum of Modern Art, 2002.

"Enlightenment comes when you don't care." Kerouac, Jack. *The Scripture of the Golden Eternity.* San Francisco: City Lights, 2001.

"You can't use up creativity . . ." Maya Angelou quoted in Ardito, Mary. "Creativity: It's the Thought That Counts." *Bell Telephone Magazine*, 61, no. 1 (1982): 32.

"There are no right answers for anything involved in art." "Rick Rubin: Legendary Music Producer, episode 275." *Lex Friedman Podcast.* April 10, 2022. Video, 2:04:16. youtube.com/watch?v=H _szemxPcTl&list=PLrAXtmErZgOdP_8GztsuKi9nrraNbKKp4&index=92.

"If you feel safe in the area you're working in . . ." "David Bowie on why you should never play to the gallery." Video, 1:00. youtube.com /watch?v=cNbnef_eXBM.

"In my writing I am acting as a mapmaker . . ." Burroughs, William S. *Word Virus: The William S. Burroughs Reader.* New York: Grove Press, 2000.

"Our task is to create memes." McKenna, Terence. "Memes, drugs and community: Terence McKenna." Audio, 7:39. youtube.com /watch?v=NO6-1sqQme0..

"If you think adventure is dangerous, try routine . . ." Coelho, Paulo (@ paulocoelho) "If you think adventure is dangerous, try routine—it is lethal." Twitter, November 14, 2011. twitter.com/paulocoelho/status /136223869823496192?s=20&t=Tz6yXOATESFu6_pNv0VFPA.

Jobs, Steve. "Stanford Commencement Address." June 12, 2005. Stanford University, Stanford, California. Prepared text and video: news.stanford.edu/2005/06/12/youve-got-find-love-jobs-says.

"I speak a new language . . ." Williams, Saul. *Said the Shotgun to the Head.* New York: Pocket Books, 2003.

"Artists . . . are the real architects of change . . ." Burroughs, William S. *Burroughs Live: The Collected Interviews of William S. Burroughs. 1960–1997*, edited by Sylvère. Los Angeles: Semiotext(e), 2002.

"Musical innovation is full of danger to the State . . ." Plato. *The Republic.* Translated by Benjamin Jowett. London: Henry Frowde, 1888.

"We cannot evolve faster than our language . . ." McKenna, Terence. This excerpt from one of McKenna's lectures is sampled in the song "Meme Magic" by Akira the Don on the *Living in the Future* album, 2018.

"In a way, it's the poets who have failed us . . ." McKenna, Terence. "Opening the Doors of Creativity." October 1990. A video and transcription of the lecture are available at the Library of Consciousness: organism.earth/library/document/opening-the-doors-of-creativity.

"We must now reach back into time for a new cultural model. . . ." McKenna, Terence. "Opening the Doors of Creativity." October 1990.

"The role of the artist is to make the revolution irresistible." Toni Cade Bambara, cited in Lewis, Thabiti, ed. *Conversations with Toni Cade Bambara.* Jackson, MS: University Press of Mississippi, 2017.

"This above all: to thine own self be true." Shakespeare, William. *Hamlet*. 1603.

"It is our mission on Earth to combat false teachings . . ." Miller, Henry. *The Time of the Assassins*. New York: New Directions, 1962.

© Bhavin Misra

ABOUT THE AUTHOR

JAMES MCCRAE is an artist, poet, and teacher who empowers creators to live with purpose and turn imagination into reality. He is the founder of Sunflower Club, a podcast and global community dedicated to creativity as a tool for personal healing and social transformation. As a creative strategist, he has worked with top brands and startups to define and actualize their message and mission. As an artist, James uses internet memes to communicate deep concepts in a simple, humorous way, which he shares on his popular Instagram page @wordsarevibrations. His books include *Sh#t Your Ego Says* and *How to Laugh in Ironic Amusement During Your Existential Crisis.* His debut album of spoken-word poetry, *Our Last Night in Los Angeles*, is available now. James lives in Austin, Texas.

Website: jamesmccrae.com

Instagram: @wordsarevibrations

Podcast: Sunflower Club

ABOUT SOUNDS TRUE

SOUNDS TRUE was founded in 1985 by Tami Simon with a clear mission: to disseminate spiritual wisdom. Since starting out as a project with one woman and her tape recorder, we have grown into a multimedia publishing company with a catalog of more than 3,000 titles by some of the leading teachers and visionaries of our time, and an ever-expanding family of beloved customers from across the world.

In more than three decades of evolution, Sounds True has maintained our focus on our overriding purpose and mission: to wake up the world. We offer books, audio programs, online learning experiences, and in-person events to support your personal growth and awakening, and to unlock our greatest human capacities to love and serve.

At SoundsTrue.com you'll find a wealth of resources to enrich your journey, including our weekly *Insights at the Edge* podcast, free downloads, and information about our nonprofit Sounds True Foundation, where we strive to remove financial barriers to the materials we publish through scholarships and donations worldwide.

To learn more, please visit SoundsTrue.com/freegifts or call us toll-free at 800.333.9185.

Together, we can wake up the world.

sounds true

WAKING UP THE WORLD